S0-BJG-207

Promoting Harmony

Young Adolescent Development and Classroom Practices

Third Edition

David Strahan, Mark L'Esperance, and John Van Hoose

National Middle School Association
Westerville Ohio

Betty Edwards, Executive Director
April Tibbles, Director of Publications
Carla Weiland, Publications Editor
John Lounsbury, Editor, Professional Publications
Edward Brazee, Consulting Editor, Professional Publications
Mary Mitchell, Designer, Editorial Assistant
Dawn Williams, Publications Manager
Lindsay Kronmiller, Cover and Layout Designer
Marcia Meade-Hurst, Senior Publications Representative
Peggy Rajala, Publications & Event Marketing Manager

National Middle School Association
4151 Executive Parkway, Suite 300
Westerville, Ohio 43081
1-800-528-NMSA f: 614-895-4750
www.nmsa.org

Dedication

To the memory of our good friend and mentor John Van Hoose, and to his unwavering advocacy for young adolescents everywhere.

Contents

Foreword

The Heart and Soul of Middle Schools
Edward N. Brazee

The premise of this book is deceptively simple—"the process of becoming a successful school begins with an understanding of young adolescents and an appreciation for their unique needs." While this sounds like the thesis of innumerable middle level articles, books, and classroom resources, *Promoting Harmony* delivers the goods. It shows how teachers, students, and parents can work together in harmony and illustrates occasions when school practices become discordant as well.

This is one reason that the original *Young Adolescent Development and School Practices: Promoting Harmony,* first published in 1988 and rewritten in 2001, has been one of National Middle School Association's best sellers for more than 20 years. With chapters on physical, sexual, intellectual, and social development, and one on the personal characteristics of young adolescents plus a concluding chapter, the book was influential in helping thousands of educators and other adults gain a real understanding of young adolescents.

This new edition will continue to educate new generations of middle level educators, parents, and other adults about young adolescents and the practices that we must put in place for schools to be both academically rigorous and developmentally responsive. The slight change in the title reflects a greater emphasis on classroom practices; practitioners will appreciate these examples of practices that are specific, useful, and yet flexible enough to be adapted to a variety of programs.

Readers new to *Promoting Harmony* will appreciate the responsive practices that demonstrate the authors' understanding of the influence of technology and the media on the social and moral development of young adolescents. Teachers familiar with the earlier edition will recognize the full understanding of young adolescent development that is portrayed in the insights and suggestions offered. Comments by young adolescents and their teachers give an intimate and much-needed perspective of the issues confronting them in our complex world.

The authors have done a superb job of searching out current research and best practices for each chapter. It is obvious that they know young adolescents; and they recognize, too, that we understand their trials and tribulations best when we hear from young adolescents themselves.

This is one of those books that should be read by every teacher and every parent of young adolescents, because it provides an understanding of 10- to 15-year-olds that is directly related to school practices not readily available elsewhere. This publication is a gold mine of ideas that can be used to make schools better places for young adolescents.

This book will significantly and positively impact the way educators, parents, and the community view young adolescents—and the classroom practices that will allow them to be successful.

March, 2009

Preface

Since National Middle School Association (NMSA) first published *Promoting Harmony* in 1988, it has been a best seller. The book's success is a tribute to John Van Hoose, whose memory makes this third edition bittersweet. When I joined the faculty of UNC Greensboro in 1984 and began to work with John, he quickly became my mentor. John was passionate about providing great schooling for young adolescents. Often asked to provide professional development, he had a knack for presenting essential ideas in an engaging fashion. He shared anecdotes about his own youth and humorous stories about his experiences as a teacher and parent. He encapsulated important insights from research in ways that captured the heart of the matter. In the mid-1980s, a number of school districts in North Carolina were implementing the middle school concept. It was a great pleasure to join John in conducting workshops designed to help teachers better understand the students they were serving.

After a few years working together, we decided it would be helpful to have a little book that summarized the important ideas. Although a growing number of research reports and textbooks offered valuable information about early adolescent development, many of them were too long for busy teachers to read. We prepared a manuscript, entitled it *Young Adolescent Development and School Practices: Promoting Harmony,* and offered it to the North Carolina Middle School Association for publication as a monograph. We sent a copy to John Lounsbury, and soon NMSA dressed it up and published it as a small book.

During the 1990s we used *Young Adolescent Development and School Practices* in our courses and workshops. Others across the country must have been doing the same thing, as it sold well. A few years later, NMSA asked us to update the book to incorporate the ever-growing body of research on youth development. John Van Hoose and I decided to invite Mark L'Esperance to work with us on the second edition. Mark was a natural choice. He had been an enthusiastic student in our program at UNC Greensboro, became an outstanding teacher at Northeast Middle School in Guilford County, and continued his studies with us, first in our masters program and then as a doctoral student. He brought fresh experience and great insight to the writing.

John, already battling cancer, committed himself to the revision and courageously stayed with it until the end. Unfortunately, just before the book's release, John Van Hoose was lost to this cruel disease.

Soon it became time to update the book again. As we discussed doing so, Mark and I decided to focus more on life in classrooms. We had collaborated on a number of studies of successful schools and effective practices. These materials would be useful in the revision. During this time period, research has increasingly emphasized the integration of developmental themes. This new edition reflects these transitions.

We have incorporated recent research into our chapters, revised the chapters to offer more interdisciplinary connections, and added new chapters that highlight our studies with inspiring teachers.
We have kept many of John's sentences and we still hear his voice in them. We have tried to keep something of his engaging style, his advocacy for youth, and his joyful spirit. We gratefully dedicate this special book to his memory.

David Strahan, March 2009

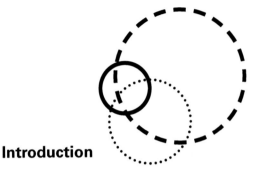

Introduction

Harmony and Discord
in the Middle Level Classroom

Nothing is real with us. You know, sometimes I'll catch myself talking to a girlfriend, and realize I don't mean half of what I'm saying. I don't really think a beer blast on the river bottom is supercool, but I'll rave about one to a girlfriend just to be saying something. She smiled at me. "I never told anyone that. I think you're the first person I've ever really gotten through to." It seems like we're always searching for something to satisfy us, and never finding it. —Cherry to Ponyboy in *The Outsiders* (Hinton, 1967)

One of the reasons for *The Outsiders'* popularity across the past four decades is the degree to which Hinton captures the emotional intensity of adolescence. Although readers may not have shared the character's experiences, many have shared the feelings expressed such as confusion, anxiety, excitement—the general sense of searching, the frustrations that come with being in the "in between years."

While many of these feelings are universal, middle grades students are often labeled with a number of stereotypes. They are "troublesome," "unpredictable," and, perhaps, "disrespectful." Some are "confused," "turned off," or "wild." Such stereotypes overlook the range of differences among students. Even so, they reflect that older view of early adolescence as a time of "storm and stress" that has characterized adolescent psychology for over a hundred years.

Certainly early adolescence is a time that encompasses a great range of developmental changes. The physical changes are dramatic. Sexual changes often have emotional impact. Social challenges consume time and energy, as do experiments with new ways of thinking. Understanding young adolescents in general and individuals in particular becomes increasingly important as we consider the changing demographics of our youth. Intrator and Kunzman (2009) reported that the 40 million adolescents ages 10–19 in the United States were already more racially and ethnically diverse than the older population. By the year 2020, this portion of the population will be 56 percent white, 23 percent Hispanic, 14 percent African American, 6 percent Asian/Pacific Islander, and 1 percent Native American.

Considering youth by categories and numbers can create serious misperceptions, however. In her analysis of the "sociocultural constructions of adolescence," Alvermann (2009) raised the possibility that concepts of youth as separate and distinct from adults create risks of misunderstanding. "It also limits what teachers, researchers, and policymakers can learn from students' experiences, at least to the extent that students are willing to share their perceptions of those experiences" (p. 25). Alvermann's caution echoes Mee's (1997) conclusion that "young adolescents are more than simply that portion of the population going through puberty. They comprise a particularly critical group as they travel from childhood to adolescence and then into young adulthood, making decisions that determine the nature of their futures" (p. 1).

The complexity of the changes that occur during early adolescence has convinced us that a successful middle level school has to be designed to meet the unique needs of its particular students. Because these needs are so dynamic, the school culture must be responsive and supportive.

In many ways, a successful school is like a symphony. As the harmonizing of many parts results in powerful music, so, too, the appropriate blending of many factors in a school results in powerful experiences for students. Like symphonies, each successful school is different. Each group of students, each staff, and each set of dynamics interact to create unique climates for learning. This interaction of factors is especially critical in the middle grades. Studies of successful middle schools acknowledge the complexity of the interactions. The outcomes of their success are like beautiful music. While they capture our attention and draw us close, the underlying "score" is more difficult to describe.

A common theme is clear. Successful middle schools meet the developmental needs of their students. In its landmark position paper *This We Believe: Successful Schools for Young Adolescents* (2003), National Middle School Association stated "For middle schools to be successful, their students must be successful; for students to be successful, the school's organization, curriculum, pedagogy, and programs must be based upon the developmental readiness, needs, and interests of young adolescents. This concept is at the heart of middle level education" (p. 1). Teaching that is developmentally responsive is the underlying focus of *Promoting Harmony*. Responsiveness creates the harmony of the symphony. In the most successful schools, instructional decisions are based on the needs of the students; and the notes, in harmony, produce wonderful music.

However, not all decisions made or all interactions that take place in all middle schools are harmonious. Some decisions, activities, and events reflect discord. They conflict with the needs of students and disrupt the flow of the music. Some of these noises are minor irritants. They create a "static" that is distracting. Other noises are more disturbing. They promote disharmony, and if accumulated, create such a cacophony that we no longer hear the music. Over time, these episodes can create so much discord that some students become disenchanted and, perhaps, tune out altogether.

This third and considerably enlarged edition continues to explore the "harmony" and "disharmony" of events in the middle grades. Previous editions (1988; 2001) have highlighted ways that successful middle level schools respond to the needs of their students. More than two decades have passed since the first edition. Since then, events and innovations have impacted the way schools function. Tragic events involving the use of weapons in schools along with the rising juvenile crime rate have required schools to rethink the issue of school safety. Intense pressures from federal, state, and local officials to raise achievement test scores have forced principals and teachers to rethink curriculum, instruction, and assessment practices. Technology is progressing at such a rapid rate that teachers are often receiving on-site staff development from their students, who often possess both the skills and hardware that are more current than what exists in the schools.

Television and the media continue to have a tremendous influence on the social and moral development of adolescents. Society, culture, populations, and individuals continually evolve and grow, for better or worse; yet the essence of adolescence remains suspended in time. Somehow, through all this, adolescents continue to be adolescents. While their world is different, they encounter the same developmental issues faced by their older brothers and sisters—and even, to some extent, by their parents. These predictable patterns of experience have created "wisdom of practice" among successful middle level teachers, perhaps best summarized in a recent review of research that concluded "young adolescents deserve educational experiences and schools that are organized to address their unique physical, intellectual, emotional/ psychological, moral/ethical, and social developmental characteristics and needs" (Caskey & Anfara, 2007, p. 4).

Among the many changes that have occurred since the 2001 edition of *Promoting Harmony,* one of the most encouraging shifts has been the consensus regarding the power of responsive middle level practice. The wisdom of practice that evolved over time has now been substantiated by comprehensive, longitudinal studies that document the impact of the middle school concept. One of the best syntheses of this research and experience is *This We Believe in Action: Implementing Successful Middle Level Schools* edited by Tom Erb. In the chapter entitled "In perspective—After 32 years of advocacy, what have we learned?" Edward Brazee and John Lounsbury provide a concise summary of this research:

> The now established research that supports the validity of the middle school concept is substantial and clear (Backes, Ralston, & Ingwalson, 1999; Felner, Jackson, Kasak, Mulhall, Brand, & Flowers, 1997; Flowers, Mertens, & Mulhall, 2003; Lee & Smith, 1993; Picucci, Brownson, Kahlert, & Sobel, 2004). The research-based generalization that evolves, simply stated is: Those schools that implement the tenets of *This We Believe* faithfully over time report improvements in students' academic achievement and in their overall development as persons. (p. 175)

Because the case for responsive middle level schools is now so strong and the documentation of successful school practices so detailed, we have focused this edition on successful classroom practices. Our slightly revised title, *Promoting Harmony: Young Adolescent Development and Classroom Practices* reflects our shift in emphasis. In this edition we continue to examine the essence of adolescence in an era of dramatic change. We first present the highlights of our updated findings about the developmental needs of students and relate this information to classroom practices. We describe the "harmony" that is generated when students' needs are addressed and the "discord" that is produced when events conflict with those needs. To ensure that what we say is grounded in the realities of early adolescence, we include a series of vignettes that convey what middle level students and teachers think and feel. These glimpses of the life in middle level schools are actual excerpts from a series of formal and informal interviews we conducted with students and teachers.

When the vignettes convey harmony, this symbol will be used:

 Harmony

When the vignette represents discord, this symbol will be used:

 Discord

Finally, when the interview comments simply shed light on the realities of what it is like to live as a young adolescent, this symbol will be used:

 Reality

We believe this publication will serve educators well and provide a firm basis for examining and improving classroom practices. We hope that readers will increasingly be in harmony as they direct the learning and development of young adolescents and, perhaps, have a better ear for detecting and countering disharmony when it appears.

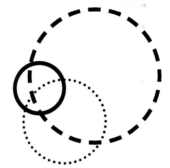

Chapter 1

Moments of Harmony: Relationships as the Essence of Good Teaching

A successful middle level school proactively addresses the unique needs of the young adolescents who attend that school. Because these needs are so dynamic, good middle level teachers are responsive and supportive. In this chapter, we focus more specifically on ways successful teachers create classroom environments that promote harmony.

While we have used a musical metaphor, teachers have described these moments of harmony in many ways. Some talk about times "when everything goes together." Others refer to "being in the zone." Years ago, a teacher described these times as "aha moments":

> When I am teaching a lesson, I watch students' eyes to see if the picture is growing clear. When I see those pictures in their eyes, that is the "aha moment" for me. If I see the picture begin

to fade, I know I have to adjust my lesson to bring the pictures back. That's the excitement that keeps me going.

Psychological researchers use the language of "flow" to describe these times when learning occurs most naturally (Csikszentmihalyi, 1990). Csikszentmihalyi and his colleagues (1989) have found that adolescents' involvement in meaningful learning activities is characterized by "flow."

> Flow is what people feel when they enjoy what they are doing, when they would not want to do anything else. What makes flow so intrinsically motivating? The evidence suggests a simple answer: in flow, the human organism is functioning at its fullest capacity. When this happens, the experience is its own reward. (p. 55)

We will explore concepts of flow more specifically in Chapter 2. In this chapter, we explore the dynamics of harmony in the classroom.

A growing body of research has identified relationships as the single most important variable in school success. In the summer of 2003, the Center for Adolescent Health and Development at the University of Minnesota coordinated an extensive review of research on factors essential to success in school (Blum, 2005). They then invited an interdisciplinary group of educational leaders to meet at the Wingspread Conference Center and make recommendations based on this research. The resulting document entitled "The Wingspread Declaration: A National Strategy for Improving School Connectedness" concluded,

> Students are more likely to succeed when they feel connected to school. School connection is the belief by students that adults in the school care about their learning as well as about them as individuals. The critical requirements for feeling connected include students' experiencing
>
> - High academic expectations and rigor coupled with support for learning.
> - Positive adult-student relationships.
> - Physical and emotional safety. (p. 20)

In their synthesis of studies entitled "Who Are Adolescents Today? Youth Voices and What They Tell Us," Intrator and Kunzman (2009) reported results from more than a dozen investigations that document ways that students view relationships with teachers and classmates as the most important factor in their learning. "Across the studies we reviewed, youth express the perception that adults who can engage them in supportive and affirmative relationships matter in how they experience the curriculum" (p. 39). In one of the most intensive of the studies they reviewed, Cushman (2003) conducted focus groups, informal discussions, and debates with 40 students from across the country. She also analyzed a wide range of writing samples. From these data, she concluded: "Our groups offered surprisingly little critique of curriculum and assessment. They focused more on the relationships that made learning possible" (p. xii as cited in Intrator & Kunzman, 2009, p. 40).

Students view relationships with teachers and class-mates as the most important factor in their learning.

 Harmony

Teacher: When you notice that one of your students comes to school with a new haircut, you've got to be careful. It's like playing "Russian Roulette." If you bring attention to a student and give a compliment in front of his or her peers, you may get a positive response or in some cases group laughter. This can be devastating to anyone, never mind a 13-year-old whose self-concept is so fragile. I've always taken the approach that to be safe, any such compliment should be given in relative privacy.

In some schools we have visited, we have not seen teachers talking with students informally before school or between classes. Teachers congregate in the lounge or stay to themselves. In one extreme situation, we observed a teacher who grabbed a student by the neck and stood him against the lockers because he happened to walk between two teachers who were talking.

 Discord

Eighth grade male: I would also get rid of the hateful school secretary. There is one at my school that the kids call the dragon lady. She will snap your head off if you have to go into the office for any reason. I hate to have to go in there with a note from home if I have to go the doctor or somewhere. She hates kids.

Furrer and Skinner (2003) analyzed specific ways that students' perceptions of their relationships with other people contributed to their engagement in lessons and their success in school. Researchers collected extensive survey data from 641 students in grades three through six on three measures: self-reported engagement, relatedness to others (parents, teachers, peers), and beliefs about strategies for success in school. They analyzed these data in relationship to teachers' ratings of students' effort, attention, and persistence during learning activities. Results demonstrated the power of positive relationships with teachers. Students who viewed themselves as less related to their teachers had lower teacher and self-reports of engagement, even when reporting strong relationships with parents and peers (p. 157). The researchers concluded, "children's sense of relatedness plays an important role in their academic motivation and performance" (p. 158).

Considering these results, Furrer and Skinner (2003) emphasized the natural logic of the evidence as a fundamental aspect of human nature:
Feelings of belonging may have an energetic function, awakening enthusiasm, interest, and willingness to participate in academic activities. It seems to be more fun for children to be involved in activities with people that they like and by whom they feel liked in return. Relatedness may also buffer against negative emotions, minimizing feelings of boredom, anxiety, pressure, or frustration. (p. 158)

Eighth grade female: My homeroom teacher is my favorite teacher. She is always nice in the morning when you come in. On Mondays she always asks about our weekends and tells us what she and her husband did. She knows a lot about plants and has spider plants all over the classroom. One time she brought in an orange cactus. A boy accidentally knocked it off the cabinet, and all the dirt went everywhere. He was really scared that he was going to get in trouble 'cause she likes plants and all, but she just laughed and said it was her fault for putting it in someone's way. Then the boy laughed too, and they cleaned it up. The next day she brought the cactus back in new dirt and got the boy to find a safe place for it. At the end of the year she gives her plants away.

In the next section of this chapter, we will review research that helps us understand these dynamics more specifically in classroom settings. The rest of this chapter is adapted from portions of the article "How Successful Teachers Develop Academic Momentum with Reluctant Students" (Strahan, 2008).

Creating personal and academic momentum

Classroom-specific studies show that our most accomplished middle level teachers develop supportive relationships with students by creating personal and academic "momentum" (Strahan, 2008). In the physical sciences, momentum is "a strength or force that keeps growing" (Webster's New World College Dictionary, 1997)). Athletes and coaches talk of momentum in sports. Advertisers try to create momentum for new products. Politicians try to strengthen momentum for candidates and ideas.

In school settings, momentum is the strength of a student's engagement with learning activities. Students with strong personal momentum interact with other people with self-assurance. Students with strong

5

academic momentum approach new assignments with confidence. Based on previous experiences, they know they are likely to do well. If something proves to be difficult, they know they have a repertoire of skills and strategies they can employ. These beliefs provide a stronger sense of identity. Students who experience success in school see themselves as more capable and more responsible.

Students with little personal and academic momentum show little confidence and doubt their abilities to do well. In some cases, they have internalized a sense of inadequacy that makes it very difficult to invest effort in new experiences. To observers, they may appear "unmotivated," "turned off," or "disconnected." These perceptions may fuel a negative sense of identity, leading to stronger feelings of inferiority.

Discord

Some students experience the factory model school day that is much like an assembly line. They "check in" to a homeroom that is little like a home, report quickly to their first class, jump and run at the sound of the bells, perform a long series of routine activities, stand at attention in long lunch lines, return quickly to an afternoon of more of the same, and run home as fast as they can when the final bell rings.

Successful teachers encourage momentum with students in various ways. In developmental language, momentum is the integration of "skill" and "will." For some time, researchers have used these constructs to describe how students achieve success in school.

Since the 1980s research has focused on how motivational and cognitive factors interact and influence student learning and achievement. It is clear that students need both the cognitive skills and the motivational will to do well in school. (Linneback & Pintrich, 2002, p. 313)

To learn new concepts, students need the will to want to understand how best to invest their energies in the learning process (Zimmerman,

6

1989; McCombs & Marzano, 1990; Linnenbrink & Pintrich, 2002). For example, a student who has done well in school will approach a difficult homework assignment with an expectation to understand what she reads, believing she can figure out the meaning of the text. If she gets confused, she may employ strategies she has learned to make sense of the material. She might ask herself questions, re-read passages, or take a brief break and return to the task with determination. These strategies give her the will to persist to meet her goal of understanding the material. In similar fashion, a student with previous success in social relationships approaches new situations with an expectation of success and the skills for creating positive relationships.

Students can be very effective in directing the learning of their classmates.

Researchers have identified two connected ways of thinking that create skill and will. Students who do well have developed self-efficacy—they believe they can perform academic and social tasks. They have also internalized a high level of self-regulation, believing they can control the factors necessary to perform the task. Many studies have documented how the development of self-efficacy and self-regulation strengthens competence (Zimmerman, Bonner, & Kovach, 1996: Paris & Paris, 2001; Linneback & Pintrich, 2002; Schunk, 2003).

These studies describe ways that young adolescents gain momentum. Students need self-efficacy to choose to engage in challenging tasks and to persist when learning becomes more difficult. Self-efficacy is not a general belief. It is task specific and based on actual accomplishments. For example, a student might believe he can solve computational problems in his math class. When he sees that the problems require addition, subtraction, multiplication, or division, he invests a great deal of energy in solving them, even as they grow more complex. If he has less self-efficacy about solving equations however, he may give up at an early stage of deliberation.

7

Momentum also requires the internalization of the skills of self-regulation. These skills connect self-observation, self-evaluation, goal setting and strategic planning, and monitoring. By examining their own responses, successful students identify ways they want to improve. They then use specific study strategies to try to reach these goals. Based on their progress, they adjust their work plans to improve their performance. When students set meaningful, realistic goals and accomplish them, they become more confident in their abilities as students and assume more responsibility for their learning. This integration of skill and will greatly accelerate academic progress.

Harmony

Observer: Jennifer is a bright, loud, beautiful eighth grade girl. She is the focal point of attention. She wrote a very poignant poem during a language arts exercise. It centered around the recent divorce of her parents and the emptiness of going home to a house half-full with siblings. It was a real "gut-wrencher" to see how this pain has forced a child to reckon with "living grief." Many of the children know about Jennifer's family problems and defended her in a conflict with a teacher. It was wise of the teacher to back down from the conflict and to give Jennifer space. Other teachers are having trouble with Jennifer. The quickest way to diffuse a situation is to not argue, banter, or push. A better time when the child is rational will come.

Nurturing academic momentum

Teachers play an essential role in nurturing students' integration of skill and will. Joyce, Wolf, and Calhoun (1993) concluded that successful teaching begins with the establishment of supporting relationships: "the literature is full of examples of teachers enabling students, even the most unlikely ones, to learn to outstanding degrees and reach beyond prediction to a self-confident, socially committed state of growth" (p. ix).

8

Such relationships are especially important when students have rarely experienced academic success. Years ago, we had an opportunity to examine the perceptions of a group of students who entered seventh grade with very little academic momentum and "bounced back" to do well that year (Strahan, 1988). We gathered work samples and interviews from a team of seventh graders across an entire school year. At the end of the year, we compared the responses of students who made progress with a matched group of students on the same team who did not make progress. Students who made little progress made few connections with the academic life of their school. When reflecting on their responses to lessons, they expressed a "survival orientation," describing ways that they tried to look busy or ask for help. Some took pride in creating disruptions, "getting into it" with classmates and teachers as a way to avoid work. In contrast, students who made progress reported functional strategies for completing assignments and tried to avoid getting in trouble. They attributed their success to their supportive relationships with their teachers and to academic tasks they could accomplish.

 Discord

Interviewer: You had a real problem in Mrs. M's class with Bobby the other day. What was that all about?

Eighth grade male: Bobby's a real wise guy. Last year he was bigger than me and was pushing me around. Well, this year I got bigger than him. I let him know that he couldn't push me around anymore, so he mouths off in class to me, and I get into trouble for talking 'cause they don't see him. Well, Mrs. M. jumped on me for talking in class, and Bobby started to laugh at me, so I gave him a kick as I went past him to sharpen my pencil. Mrs. M. caught me and sent me to the office. Next thing I know I spent the rest of the day in I.S.S. and the next day too. But that's all right. Bobby won't mess with me anymore.

Since that 1988 study, we have analyzed these dynamics in greater detail. A series of case studies with teachers who have been successful in challenging settings showed how they developed strong working rapport with students (Strahan, Smith, McElrath, & Toole, 2001). Teachers in these case studies demonstrated warm, supportive relationships based on a deep knowledge of individual students. Not only could they describe in detail the emotional, physical, cognitive, intellectual, and family needs and circumstances of students in their classes, they addressed these needs by responding to students as individuals. A longitudinal study (Strahan & Layell, 2006) chronicled ways that one middle school team accomplished success across a school year. Students on this team made significant growth, higher than that of the school as a whole. Results documented three main ways this team promoted academic achievement. Teachers 1) created a climate of shared responsibility through team building and positive discipline, 2) taught explicit strategies for performing academic tasks, and 3) developed activities that linked inquiry, collaboration, and real-world experiences.

These accomplishments are only possible when teachers have created a climate of trust. Goddard, Tschannen-Moran, and Hoy (2001) examined ways that learning depends on trust, especially in regard to language. Data from 47 elementary schools showed that measures of trust consistently predicted achievement differences in mathematics and reading, even when they controlled for race, gender, socioeconomic status, and past achievement. The authors concluded that "when teachers believe their students are competent and reliable, they create learning environments that facilitate academic success. When students trust their teachers, they are more likely to take the risks that new learning entails" (p. 14). Unfortunately, when the opposite dynamics occur, a "self-reinforcing spiral of blame and suspicion" hampers student achievement (p. 15).

A teacher provided a negative role model when the superintendent invited one of the authors on a "walking tour" that included visits to classrooms. One teacher told us that the reason this class was working at a more basic level in reading was that "All of these students are slow." She made this unsolicited comment in front of the students and they heard it. This comment was certainly insensitive and disrespectful. When adults model this type of destructive behavior, it makes it more likely for students to engage in behavior that is hurtful to each other.

To explore ways that teachers might rekindle trust with students who have struggled in school, Smith-McIlwain (2005) conducted an intensive case study with a ninth grade teacher and seven of her students. Based on observations, interviews, and analysis of writing samples, Smith-McIlwain identified three types of care that contributed to trusting relationships with students who gained academic momentum:

- Discovery talk—conversation aimed at discovering the details of students' personal lives in order to extend understanding in the classroom and "just to find out if everything is okay."
- Help—two types of help: help for personal problems and the instructional help that enables students to improve academically.
- Friendly listening—aimed at discovering personal issues that may affect classroom behaviors and academic performance.

Because she spent a great deal of time in conversations with participating students about the papers they were writing, Smith-McIlwain was able to document what she called "watershed events," which she defined as "specific events that provided the opportunity for the extension of care that resulted in the establishment of a positive personal relationship between teacher and student" (p. 10). For example, one of the participants in her study rarely completed an essay or revealed much of his thinking in writing conferences. One day, in a meeting with this student, the teacher shifted discussion away from his paper to ask about a reference he made to a family event. After sharing some of his family story, he asked the teacher to suggest ways he could write about these events in his paper. He began to talk specifically about his essay and completed it in a few days. This was his first complete paper. After that, he participated in writing conferences and submitted papers regularly. His writing began to improve. Smith-McIlwain identified that conversation about his family as a watershed event.

As this study progressed, trust promoted positive actions toward improving performance and diminished the fear of risk. Students became aware of the types of care they expected from their teacher and described them explicitly. Once this trust was in place, students expected the teacher to provide an honest assessment of their writing and to follow it with specific suggestions. Smith-McIlwain concluded that caring relationships were key to re-engaging disengaged learners more than any specific instructional practice or classroom procedure.

When considered together, these studies help us better understand the dynamics of momentum. Students who have struggled with social relationships or schoolwork have often experienced a vicious cycle of poor performance and limited effort. With few successes, they have limited "skill" to invest in new tasks and little "will" to take the risk necessary to improve their skill. Learning to trust a teacher seems to be the only way to break this cycle. When a student learns to trust a caring teacher, he or she can begin to take chances, find the will to invest effort in new challenges, and receive the help needed to improve skills. Trusting relationships thus constitute a "threshold" of action, a point beyond which meaningful learning can occur.

Harmony—the student-centered staff

Teachers in successful schools make it a point to find opportunities to talk with students outside of class. We have seen teachers seated on their desks surrounded by students before homeroom begins. We have seen them walking with students, eating lunch with students, playing basketball or chess with students, even singing songs. One school we visited conducts weekend outings several times each year. These outings are not only field trips, but social events as well, a chance for any student who wishes to take part in the community of the school.

 Harmony

Eighth grade female: Miss T has a great sense of humor. She doesn't mind if you laugh as long as it is not at someone else. You can't laugh though when she is teaching something new, then she is real serious 'cause she knows it is important. You can tell Miss T really likes us 'cause she is always asking us what we think about certain things. You can go to her if you have a problem with a friend or something, and she won't tell anyone. She understands that things are hard sometimes and that some days are just bad. If she gets mad at you for something, she doesn't stay mad for long. She will talk to you and then be nice again. Nobody wants to make Miss T mad, 'cause she is real nice to everybody.

Conclusions

The research reported in this chapter describes how successful teachers create learning communities that invite students to trust them and trust each other. Successful teachers engage students in conversations that enable them to learn more about young adolescents as individuals, understand their personal and academic strengths, and listen actively to them. As students learn to trust their teachers and their classmates, they cross a threshold. They begin to engage more frequently in lesson activities, especially those that scaffold instruction and teach strategies explicitly. Because they trust their teachers and their classmates, students begin to assess their own work more candidly and seek guidance from their teachers more willingly. They interact more positively with other people. From these successes, they begin to set goals, make plans, and assess their progress more specifically. As they gain confidence, students begin to experiment with new learning behaviors, thoughts, and feelings until they reach a point where they have enough self-efficacy and self-regulation to learn more independently.

These accomplishments have immediate impact. Students experience greater success with assignments. More importantly, they begin to see themselves as more capable and responsible, perceptions that can fuel a growing sense of identity. In the chapters that follow, we look specifically at the developmental transitions of early adolescence that make these dynamics so important.

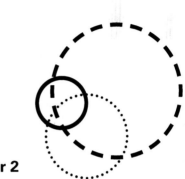

Chapter 2

Intellectual and Emotional Development

While not as visible as the physical changes, the intellectual and emotional changes that occur during early adolescence are equally dramatic. Just as muscles grow and develop new powers of movement, students' brains change and develop new powers of reasoning. They begin to think of themselves and the world around them in new ways. Their emotions grow stronger—and sometimes more confusing. For the first time in their lives, young adolescents can "think about thinking." Classroom activities play a major role in bringing about these significant intellectual and emotional changes that occur in this period. When teachers understand how reasoning develops and can interpret students' responses accordingly, they can orchestrate activities in ways that promote harmony.

In this chapter, we consider intellectual and emotional development comprehensively. Recent research studies make it clear that the notion of "feelings vs. thoughts" is outdated. Emotional thoughts are intertwined with other modes of reasoning. Goleman's (1995; 1998) studies of the relationships among ideas and feelings have highlighted many of the connections.

> In reality, the brain's wetware is awash in a messy, pulsating puddle of neurochemicals, nothing like the sanitized, orderly silicon that has spawned the guiding metaphor for mind.
>
> (Goleman, 1998, pp. 40-41)

Researchers studying the human brain are finding many ways that the brain develops across the lifespan. This does not mean that middle school students cannot think well or control their emotions—far from it. It means that one of our most important responsibilities is to help them think better. In this chapter we will explore ways that middle school students develop their minds and how this impacts their understanding of themselves and their world.

Understanding how students think

As an organizing framework for understanding more about how young adolescents think, we build on a powerful synthesis of research on learning prepared by Patricia Cross in 1999. In her monograph entitled *Learning Is About Making Connections,* Cross summarized much of what scientists have discovered about how people learn.

> Stunning new research on the brain by neuroscientists is adding a new dimension to our knowledge about learning that reinforces our previously tentative conclusions from cognitive psychology. This research provides growing evidence that learning is about making connections—whether the connections are established by firing synapses in the brain, the "ah ha" experience of seeing the connections between two formerly isolated concepts, or the satisfaction of seeing the connections between an abstraction and a "hands-on" concrete application. (p. 5)

In the decade since Cross reported her synthesis, additional research has strengthened her conclusion that learning occurs in four intertwined types of connections:

16

- Neurological connections
- Cognitive connections
- Social connections
- Experiential connections. (p. 7)

These four categories provide organizers for our analysis of intellectual development during early adolescence. After examining these four interrelated dimensions, we will explore how emotional aspects of reasoning shape our thoughts.

Neurological connections

Scientific studies on the structure of the brain are helping us understand the basic, physical nature of the connections we make when we think. Robert Leamnson (1999), a professor of biology at University of Massachusetts, described how our brains function as synaptic connections:

> The paths that signals take as they pass from one part of the brain to another are, to the nonspecialist, simply bewildering. They fan out, converge, loop back, reenter the path from multiple sites, and probably do much more that we don't know yet. (p. 12)

These multiple connections among neurons link perception and thought. Pinker (1997) describes how our minds have evolved using these neurological connections:

> The mind is what the brain does, specifically, the brain processes information and thinking is a kind of computation. . . . The mind is a system of organs of computation, designed by natural selection to solve the kinds of problems our ancestors faced in their foraging way of life, in particular, understanding and outmaneuvering objects, animals, plants, and other people. (p. 21)

Recognizing this complexity requires us to abandon outmoded metaphors for thinking. Notions such as a "blank slate" or an "empty vessel" make no sense when we understand more about the mind. "We need ideas that capture the ways a complex device can tune itself to unpredictable aspects of the world and take in the kinds of data it needs to function" (p. 33).

Caskey and Ruben (2007) summarized ways that the neurological structure of the brain changes during early adolescence. Although the brain has grown to nearly adult size by age six, the period that follows is one of "neural pruning," a process that "appears to eliminate unused connections and solidify brain circuitry" (p. 64). This process peaks dramatically in early adolescence. Another essential change is an increase in "myelination," the insulation of axons that speeds the transmission of electrical impulses from neuron to neuron (p. 64). While these physiological processes increase the efficiency of brain functions, key portions of the brain do not mature until late adolescence. One area is the prefrontal cortex, the region that serves "executive functions including planning, reasoning, anticipating consequences, sustaining attention, and making decisions" (p. 64). Another area that matures later is the hippocampus, which guides central memory and emotional reasoning. It is this region that fully engages the adult brain in the most sophisticated learning processes.

Drawing from her unique perspective as both a neurologist and a middle school teacher, Willis (2007) reported results of neuroimaging and neurochemical investigations as they relate to learning activities. She describes ways that the amygdala region of the brain responds to instructional experiences. When excessive challenges create undue stress, the amygdala becomes hyperactive, blocking information from flowing naturally through neural circuitry and making it difficult to think clearly. In contrast, when engaged with activities that produce emotional satisfaction, the metabolic activity of the brain accelerates and thinking becomes more constructive.

As neuroimaging evidence has shown, the more a student is engaged in a learning activity, especially one with multiple sensory modalities, the more parts of the brain are actively stimulated. When this occurs in a positive emotional setting, without stress and anxiety, the result is greater long-term, relational, and retrievable learning. (p. 7)

18

While it may not be wise to draw definite conclusions from this growing body of neurological research, three implications that good middle school teachers know intuitively seem unmistakable. One, early adolescence is a critical time for brain growth, a time in which this growth accelerates the powers of the mind. Clearly, middle level students can and do learn to think in new ways. Second, in spite of faster and more efficient neural connections, the brains of young adolescents are not yet mature, especially in areas that guide decision making and emotional control. Learning to make thoughtful decisions and understand feelings are central but difficult tasks for middle school students. Finally, new discoveries in the workings of the brain underscore the need for all of us in education to develop more sophisticated approaches to teaching. As Pinker (2007) concluded,

> Traditional education was dominated by a version of the conduit metaphor sometimes called the savings-and-loan model: the teacher dispenses nuggets of information to the pupils, who try to retain them in their minds long enough to give them back on an exam . . . it's undeniable that people retain more when they are called on to think about what they are learning. (p. 84)

 Discord

"Open your books, read chapter seven, and answer the questions." One of the least effective ways to teach is among the most common. When teachers give reading assignments like this, students have little motivation. Such assignments are inefficient. Students have little sense of purpose and tend to read very mechanically; most of them simply "look up the answers." They have no concrete experiences to serve as springboards to concepts. Studies of memory suggest that students forget most of what they read under such conditions within 24 hours.

Cognitive connections

Thinking and learning are the central issues in research on cognition. As Cross (1999) concluded,

> The parallels between the neurological brain and the working mind envisioned by cognitive scientists are quite remarkable. Modern cognitive science postulates a structure of the mind known as schema—or in plural forms, schemata, since the brain develops many schemata for different purposes. A schema is a cognitive structure that consists of facts, ideas, and associations organized into a meaningful system of relationships. (p. 8)

These cognitive connections are the essence of problem solving and creativity. In a synthesis of research on learning, Bransford, Brown, and Cocking (2000) concluded,

> Children are both problem solvers and problem generators: children attempt to solve problems presented to them and they also seek novel challenges. They refine and improve their problem-solving strategies not only in the face of failure, but also by building on prior successes. They persist because success and understanding are motivating in their own right. (p. 112)

Many of our current notions about how young people develop more sophisticated concepts reflect the influence of Piaget's stage theory of mental development. Piaget (1972) suggested that mental development occurs in four phases. Each child passes through the stages in the same sequence, but at varying times and rates. The logical operations of each stage develop from the operations of the previous stage. Within this framework, the early adolescent period is a time of transition from the "concrete operations" stage to the "formal operations" stage that may begin for some as early as the 11th year, while for others, three or even four years later. Figure 2.1 presents an overview of the transition from concrete to formal operations.

Figure 2.1
Early Adolescent Reasoning: A Time of Transition

	Age		
	7-11	**10-14**	**13-??**
Emerging abilities	Development of concrete reasoning	Developmental transitions	Development of formal operations
	Logical thinking about things	Mastery of concrete operations, experimentation with formal operations	Thinking with abstractions
	Classification	Creating theories	Hypothetical-deductive reasoning
	Conservation	Thinking about thinking	
	Arithmetic		
Difficulties	Abstract ideas	Empathy	Applications and transfer
	Complex verbal problems	Patience	
	Suspending judgments	Synthesis	

Students in the concrete operations stage develop the ability to carry out logical operations on concrete objects. They can reverse processes, distinguish concepts, and relate ideas in a serial fashion. They can thus solve mathematical or logical problems presented in concrete situations where they can manipulate material data they can see and touch. Logical operations in the abstract are more difficult.

As students enter the period of formal operations, they reason more logically about verbal statements in the absence of particular objects. "This period is characterized in general by the conquest of a new mode of reasoning, one that is no longer limited exclusively to dealing with objects or directly representable realities, but also employs 'hypotheses'" (Piaget, 1970, p. 33). During formal operations, students can begin to deal with such mathematical concepts as permutations, combinations, probabilities, and correlations. They can also begin to use language as a medium for expanding thinking. They become quite capable of providing reflections on life experiences in and out of school.

 Reality

Twelve-year-old male: During my spare time, "I just eat and watch TV. When I get bored, I just sit around and wait for my dad or bug my brother. I like shows about police and crime as well as music videos. I do my homework on the bus in the morning or if my dad remembers to ask, I'll just do a little for him to check. He's busy. I usually don't remind him to sign my planner. It's so stupid. Why do we need those things? I ain't no child. I don't like getting checked every day.

The development of formal operations is not a continuous process of development. Only when a student has learned to perform the operations of one stage can he or she pass on to the next. Moreover, differences in social environment and acquired experiences create wide variations in rates of development. While the average age for beginning formal operations is the 11th year, Piaget (1970) reported experimental studies showing as much as four years of "time lag" (p. 36). Within a given grade level, or even a given class, there will be wide variation in the developmental stages of individual pupils.

Figure 2.2 illustrates that variation. Responses from students to a verbal problem demonstrate a range of responses from Tom's random guess to Marc's very sophisticated propositional statement. Responses demonstrate stage differences as well. Christie used a concrete sequential strategy to solve the problem while Marc analyzed it in a formal way.

22

Figure 2.2

Responses of Fifth and Sixth Graders to a Reading and Thinking Problem

Problem Situation: At a meeting of the television news staff, the weather reporter was told that her material was too dull. That night she made up for it.

Good evening. Today's weather, as you have probably noticed, is different from yesterday's. If the weather is the same tomorrow as it was yesterday, the day after tomorrow will have the same weather as the day before yesterday. But if the weather tomorrow is the same as today, the day after tomorrow will have the same weather as yesterday. As you know, it's raining today, and it rained on the day before yesterday.

Question: Was it raining or clear yesterday?
(*Thinklab.* Science Research Associates, 1974)

Student Responses:

Tom: It's raining because the story implied it.

David: Clear—it said so in the story.

Evan: Clear—because it was clear every other day.

Wendy: You can't tell because she didn't say what tomorrow will be like.

Shannon: It was raining yesterday because the weather is the same as tomorrow and tomorrow is the same as today and it's raining today.

Rob: It will be clear because she said that today is raining and if she had said that tomorrow would be raining she could have said tomorrow would be the same as yesterday.

Christie:

Day before Yesterday	Yesterday	Today	Tomorrow	Day after Tomorrow
*	?	?	?	*

It was raining the day before yesterday, and it is raining today. So, yesterday was clear.

Daryl: Clear yesterday because of rain today.

Marc: If today's weather is different from yesterday's and it is raining today, it was clear yesterday.

Studies on the development of formal reasoning suggest that approximately one-third of eighth graders consistently demonstrate formal abilities (Tobin & Capie, 2006). These studies have far-reaching implications for curriculum and instruction. Some students may never move up to the level of formal reasoning, particularly if teachers do not challenge them. Middle level teachers should carefully consider the reasoning level of students when planning instruction and design lessons that will guide students in creating new connections (Brown & Canniff, 2007). More importantly, the distribution of reasoning development for a given class or grade level is very difficult to predict. Not only is there variability among students in the acquisition of formal reasoning (Woolfolk, 1998),

The variance among young adolescents in their development of formal operations calls for individual attention.

but there is some evidence that there is variability within individuals as well. Smart and Smart (1973) and Balk (1995) suggested that the development of formal operations is uneven across subject matter areas and is often situational. The adolescent may be able to think abstractly in one area but not in another. Adolescents often experience varying attention spans, demonstrating both a sense of urgency and a tendency to act as if time were not important. These variations in internal development further suggest a sense of "unevenness" in thinking.

This unevenness in thinking helps us understand the wide range of individual differences that are likely to occur in any given classroom at any given time. When we consider the level of abstraction required by many of the concepts in a middle school curriculum, instructional planning becomes even more complex. A brief sample of such concepts is listed in Figure 2.3.

Figure 2.3

A Sample of Abstract Concepts Taught in the Middle Grades

LANGUAGE ARTS
Main idea
Metaphor
Parts of Speech
Symbolism
Theme

SCIENCE
Conservation of Energy
Molecular structure
Photosynthesis
Relativity
Respiration

MATHEMATICS
Algebraic Expression
Equations
Ratio
Sets
Thought Problems

SOCIAL STUDIES
Democracy
Distance (Thousands of Miles)
Justice
Space (Countries, Continents)
Time (Centuries, Millennia)

Approaching these concepts in a meaningful way requires teachers to help students make connections between the concrete ideas they already understand and new abstractions. Teaching formal concepts without careful planning can make learning even more difficult for students.

 Discord

Thirteen-year-old male: I liked science and math. I usually got As in these subjects. This last year I took algebra. I didn't understand it. The teacher didn't explain it right. She'd go through a whole problem, give us homework, and then the next day she'd give us a test. I just didn't get it. I'm taking algebra next year again when I'm in the ninth grade.

Blanket requirements that all eighth graders take algebra may not be sound. Understanding how formal reasoning develops over time should help teachers plan instruction that encourages students to try new modes of reasoning without penalizing them for having difficulty making abstract connections. For example, Tobin and Capie (2006) analyzed the responses of 156 middle school students to science lessons

25

and found that formal reasoning ability was the strongest predictor of achievement and retention, accounting for approximately 36 percent of the variance in each case. Although middle level teachers are generally aware of the power of formal reasoning, a recent study by Brown and Canniff (2007) indicated that the curricula of many middle schools continues to require students to engage in formal operational cognitive processes, "even though most students seldom reach the levels of understanding that teachers might expect in each subject area" (p. 16).

Piaget's studies of reasoning development have helped us appreciate ways that concepts develop over time and have encouraged curriculum planners to organize ideas in a logical progression. An equally important contribution has been the understanding that thinking is constructed. As Cross (1999) noted "one of Piaget's remarkable contributions to our understanding of learning is that children's cognitive structures are not preformed but rather are constructed as a result of their own mental activity. They quite literally 'build their own minds'" (p. 9).

Gardner's (1983) widely accepted theory of multiple intelligences provided a useful framework for understanding how we develop new powers of mind. His analyses of brain functions and creative processes have documented at least eight ways of understanding. In addition to the more familiar "intelligences" such as linguistic learning, logical reasoning, and spatial development, Gardner has shown that we also use bodily-kinesthetic, musical, naturalistic, and personal intelligences. Teachers of all grades have found that Gardener's theory fits their observations of classroom learning. Consequently, the concept of multiple intelligences is now providing a framework for planning lessons that tap individual talents and involve students in learning about learning. Studies of Gardner's theory in practice (Gardner & Hatch, 1989; Gardner, 1995; Moran, Kornhaber, & Gardner, 2006) have documented successful elementary, middle, and secondary applications. In reviewing the research, Gardner (1995) identified three essential aspects of good teaching with multiple intelligences: 1) cultivating desired capabilities, 2) approaching concepts, subjects, and disciplines in a variety of ways, and 3) personalizing education (pp. 207-208).

Early adolescence is clearly a particularly critical time in the development of multiple intelligences (Strahan, 1997; Gardner, 2006). As young adolescents' powers of reasoning grow more sophisticated, they become more aware of their own unique talents and interests. Some students find they have a real talent for music, or art, or movement, or nature. Others learn that they learn best when they work with others; others do better by themselves. Many find learning is most successful through a combination of intelligences. When parents and teachers support their efforts to try out

Many students enjoy working in groups and do their best work when collaborating with others.

new ideas and new modes of reasoning, students begin to take more ownership of their learning. A key element in this progression is the growing ability to think about thinking.

Young adolescents are more aware of their thoughts than they were as children. By the time they reach middle grades, students are keenly aware of times when they do not understand things that others seem to know. In fact, when presented with mental tasks that are too difficult, they may dwell on their inability to perform them. This is especially the case when they see classmates solving problems that they cannot.

One way that this becomes an issue in the classroom is the "I could do it if I wanted to" defense mechanism. When faced with tasks that appear to be too difficult, many young adolescents say to themselves, "I could figure this out if I really wanted to but I don't want to." Such a rationalization is easier than admitting that the task is too difficult. This avoidance response prevents some students from taking academic chances. Consequently, they miss opportunities to expand their powers of reasoning, making it more likely that they will be frustrated the next time they face a similar problem. Teachers who are sensitive to this issue can help students approach challenging tasks with less fear of failure by giving time, encouragement, and support.

Seventh grade female: Math is my favorite because our teacher makes it really fun, and I learn a lot. When I was little I wasn't good in math because it was real hard, and I never could get my homework right. Now I am good in math. I usually make an A or B in it because I understand it. Our teacher is great because she explains things and doesn't mind if you ask questions, even if she has already explained it once. My math teacher's favorite subject is math. You can tell she likes it a lot because she always seems happy when we come to class. We always have homework in math, and I don't mind doing it because I can get it right without asking my mom.

One of the most helpful frameworks for understanding how young adolescents think about their thoughts is Glasser's (1998) *Choice Theory: A New Psychology of Personal Freedom*. Choice Theory describes ways that students choose their behaviors to fit their self-made pictures of themselves and to meet basic needs for security, belonging, freedom, power, and fun (Glasser, 1993, pp. 123–37). Not trying when a task seems too difficult is a way of preserving psychological security. "Not trying" in order to fit in with others who are not trying may be an attempt to belong. Sometimes, students assert themselves to bolster a sense of freedom or power. At other times, diversion seems like more fun than participation.

Glasser's studies show that students can form more productive pictures of themselves when they experience success and identify with significant others. Teachers can help students think about their thoughts more productively by encouraging them to consider choices and consequences. In sharing results from a program that implemented Choice Theory in a systematic fashion designed to encourage better decisions among students with frequent discipline referrals, Walter, Lamcie, and Ngazimbi (2008) reported that participating students demonstrated higher levels of engagement in lessons and fewer

28

discipline problems. Other programs have demonstrated similar results (Passaro, Moon, Wiest, & Wong, 2004; Kruczek, Alexander, & Harris, 2005). Taking time to identify options for decisions and predict the outcomes of these options helps students develop a stronger sense of personal responsibility and strengthens the basic cognitive connections that structure their thoughts.

 Harmony

Interviewer: Tell me about your latest work with the book the class is reading, *The Outsiders*.

Fifteen-year-old male: I take notes on the characters—they've changed me. I've been telling everyone what they're like. When they make decisions, we have to write down what decision they have to make and why they made it. For example, Dally sneaked into the movies. It only cost a quarter, but he sneaked in to show how tough he was. I could see him doing that— even though he had the money.

Social connections

Research is helping us understand how the cognitive connections we make when we think are closely intertwined with social dynamics. Cross (1999) provided a clear summary of these connections:

> Learning is neither solely "in the head," nor is knowledge an exact copy in the mind of some objective external reality. Any person's understanding of reality is filtered through that individual's past experiences and understandings and through cultural interpretations and explanations. In brief, social constructivists contend that learning consists of people's efforts to make sense of the world around them. (p. 17)

Many of the insights emerging about shared aspects of thinking have evolved from Vygotsky's social learning theories. Vygotsky (1978) described ways that intellectual development grows from observations of others and participation in collaborative activities. Social interactions—with other children and with adults—enable children to expand their prior knowledge and their use of language (Wood, Roser, & Martinez, 2001). Social learning theories emphasize two intertwined dimensions of language—language as a social tool for sharing thoughts and language as a psychological tool for constructing thoughts.

Young people naturally rely on their interactions with others as a way of making sense of the world around them. For example, when learning the latest video game, many middle schoolers will call a friend before reading the directions, even if the friend has never played the game. One of the authors once observed a group of sixth graders unpacking a new game system and loading an unfamiliar game for the first time. By pushing buttons and talking about the responses, they quickly learned the basic structure of the game. They also developed a shared language for playing the game, memorizing the names of the levels, assigning words to the moves, and creating a vocabulary for solving the problems the game presented—all without ever looking at the directions. In these natural instances, young adolescents learn new language and use that language as a tool for communicating with peers. At the same time, that language becomes a psychological tool for creating new mental connections.

Ravenscroft (2007) studied these dynamics in a carefully controlled academic study. Researchers compared the responses of 36 students ages 15 and 16 to three different learning conditions in physics. One group examined concepts in a traditional classroom setting, another group worked with a tutor in a digital dialogue game, and a third worked with peers in a similar digital dialogue game. Results showed that adding digital dialogue produced significant improvement in understanding. "Although all students had been conventionally taught the 'correct' physics, virtually all these students retained significant alternative conceptions that were only reconciled through the intervention of the dialogue games" (p. 462). This study showed how digital dialogue games can enrich academic learning and reaffirmed Ravenscroft's conviction that dialogue is essential to learning:

> Dialogue is arguably the primary medium by which we
> understand and change the way we understand the world,
> express and convey our own identities, and also form the

sort of relationships that create the spaces where learning can happen. (p. 463)

Rojas-Drummond, Albarran, and Littleton (2008) reported a study that provides specific glimpses of how social learning connections occur in the classroom. Researchers examined conversations among 56 fourth graders in Mexico City and the work products they created. In teams of three, students developed stories, first as word processing documents and then as multimedia presentations. As they did so, they talked in ways that enabled them to co-construct new ideas. In one group, for example, the writing process began with each student suggesting a different goal for the characters.

Dialogue among students helps clarify thoughts and advance ideas and the thinking of all participants.

(They) put forward three different perspectives through a 'brain-storming' process reflecting different creative proposals. These different perspectives create a tension which is eventually resolved by the children exhibiting a disposition to negotiate instead of each child trying to impose his or her own point of view. The sequencing of ideas reveals that, instead of a simple accumulation and acceptance of each other's suggestions, the children, through each turn, are also actively proposing a chaining of new ideas which enrich the ones offered previously (i.e. an undefined character becomes a gorilla, who in turn becomes grumpy, and then also bad, etc. (p. 185)

Rojas-Drummond, Albarran, and Littleton concluded that this "fruitful chaining of ideas" results in stories that are far more intricate than those that may have been constructed individually.

Studies like these help us better understand how students think together. When conversation becomes purposeful dialogue, collaboration is more than getting along nicely. It is actively interpreting, processing, and making sense of new information. These dynamics clearly integrate neurological, cognitive, and social modes of reasoning, all of which flow together in learning through experience.

Reality

Interviewer: Tell me about this last decision scenario, the one where someone is picking on one of your good friends.

Fifteen-year-old male: You could try to stop it, or you could leave it alone and let your friend deal with it. A really bad choice would be to stand up and start something with them. You should try to get them to stop and leave your friend alone, because later down the road, your friend will be able to help you. Sometimes I would try to stop it, or I would stand up and start something, because they've got no right to pick on someone, it ain't right. What's hard is you don't want to get in a fight and get kicked out of school—but you don't want to see your friend made fun of. So, either way you go, you get hurt. Sometimes when you tell them to stop, they'll start on you.

Experiential connections

Cross (1999) described two essential dimensions of experiential learning:

First is the pedagogical use of experience to improve learning, and second is the use of learning to improve performance. In the first instance, we say that "experience is the best teacher," implying that one can learn from experience. In the second way of connecting experience and learning, we say that we want an education that is useful—one that will lead to improved performance. Students—and more broadly speaking, the American public, want an education that is "relevant," one that provides knowledge that can be used. (p. 20)

Flow theory (Csikszentmihalyi, 1990) cited in Chapter 1, provides a powerful framework for understanding how individuals learn through experience and is repeated here.

32

Csikszentmihalyi and his colleagues (1989) have found that adolescents' involvement in meaningful learning activities is characterized by "flow."

Flow is what people feel when they enjoy what they are doing, when they would not want to do anything else. What makes flow so intrinsically motivating? The evidence suggests a simple answer: in flow, the human organism is functioning at its fullest capacity. When this happens, the experience is its own reward. (p. 55)

In a series of studies conducted with people of all ages from several different parts of the world, Csikszentmihalyi and his research team observed that almost everyone shares some notion of the concept of "flow." While the nature of the tasks may vary by age range or interest, all of the people profiled have reported times when they were so involved in a task that they lost track of time. This feeling of immersion, whether in reading a book, climbing a mountain, playing a musical instrument or watching a movie, is the essential definition of flow. Participants in these studies have shared stories of being so engaged with the moment at hand that they forget to take a break to eat or failed to remember something important they were supposed to do. These moments of immersion characterize flow as one of the most powerful states of mind.

Moments of immersion occur when a group is intent on playing a content-oriented game.

In one of their most intensive studies, Csikszentmihalyi and his colleagues studied the daily life of adolescents over a 12-year period. They asked participants to record their thoughts and feelings when prompted by beepers that were programmed to go off at random intervals. During each week of the study, researchers gathered from 30 to 50 "snapshots of daily life" that they used as a basis for extended interviews with their participants. The resulting analysis delineated over 100 different activities that adolescents viewed as enjoyable.

The resulting "flow model" of intrinsic motivation describes key factors that interact to produce (or inhibit) cognitive engagement. Csikszentmihalyi (1990) summarized some of the ways that fifth and sixth graders reported "flow experiences:"

> One after the other, these children described what they enjoyed most about playing the piano, or swimming, or acting in the school plays. One said that while doing these things, "I can forget my problems." Another said, "I can keep the things that bother me out of my mind" and so on. In class, they claimed, they could seldom achieve such concentration. (p. 130)

 Discord

Interviewer: Tell me about the rain forest unit that you just completed.

Sixth grade female: I was glad that I had been to some real rain forests—when we got to go to Hawaii and when the Girl Scouts did our geo-caching trip to the park. It was really cool— we had to use the GPS to find stuff. I wish we could have talked about those things, but we just kept cutting out leaves for display night. Next time, they should have a leaf cutter.

In the classroom, students reported a "vicious circle" of experiences in which they sometimes were not concentrating on the tasks at hand, began to think of other things, and then found it even more difficult to concentrate. Consequently, "even in very good schools students actually pay attention to what is supposed to go on quite rarely" (p. 134). Csikszentmihalyi concluded that flow experiences in academic settings require a sense of "immersion" in the tasks themselves (p. 137). Teachers who "intuitively know that the best way to achieve their goals is to enlist students' interest on their side" and who "do this by being sensitive to students' goals and interests" have the best chance of encouraging such immersion (p. 137).

They empower students to take control of their learning; they provide clear feedback to the students' efforts without making them self-conscious. They help students concentrate and get immersed in the symbolic world of the subject matter. (p. 137)

Csikszentmihalyi insisted that teachers play an essential role in encouraging enjoyment.

Basically, young people are influenced by adults who appear to enjoy what they do, and who promise to make the youth's life more enjoyable too. This is not such a bad yardstick to use— why should youth choose models who seem miserable and who strive to impoverish their future? (p. 133)

By understanding more about the nature of students' thoughts when they are naturally engaged in a flow state of mind, teachers can encourage more powerful modes of reasoning.

Such understanding is especially important as today's youth experience a wide variety of interactions with "nonprint" media. Recent reviews of research studies document ways that the changing nature of information itself affects the ways young people think (Alvermann, 2009; Intrator & Kunzman, 2009). Bruce (2009) provided a rich portrayal of the sophisticated types of reading, composing, and reasoning that many young adolescents demonstrate with nonprint media. His review of 15 studies of adolescents' interactions with media literacy showed they have high levels of understanding, strong critical thinking, and elaborate composition skills when using video, music, online conversation, advertisements, television, film, comic books, video games, and magazines. "None of the studies showed students being reluctant to engage with some form of media" (p. 300).

To illustrate the complexity of some of the reasoning employed, Bruce presented a case study conducted with his nephew Jonathon "who is conscientious about his schoolwork, though it really is just something to finish so he can send time on his real interest: skateboarding" (p. 288). Jonathon reads skateboarding magazines, plays skateboarding video games, searches the Internet for videos, and creates his own videos to share. He has become an accomplished videographer, studying videos to learn about skateboarding skills and to extend his knowledge of this craft. Bruce described his careful attention to detail, his creativity in composing and editing, and his incredible attention span.

> It is noteworthy that Jonathon spent 18 hours in one day to compose this video. I taught high school English and media studies for 11 years prior to working in higher education. Though I remember a number of students postponing writing assignments until the last possible moment before cramming to get them done, I cannot recall a single student who voluntarily spent 18 ours in a day writing anything with print. (p. 290)

Bruce (2009), Alvermann (2009), Intrator and Kunzman (2009), and others documented a wide range of ways that young adolescents reason differently in their lives outside of school than they do during the confines of classrooms. In many cases, their reasoning is richer and deeper than what the curriculum asks of them. Teachers who find ways to integrate various literacies with content area learning are incorporating these talents to enrich a broader spectrum of academic understanding (Langer, 2009; Rhodes & Robnolt, 2009; Zoss, 2009). As we learn more about how to connect the talents students bring to learning outside the classroom with the demands of the curriculum within, we can foster conditions that encourage the experiential and emotional aspects of learning.

Emotional development

As researchers have discovered new insights about ways of thinking and powers of introspection, a number of studies have underscored the importance of emotions in the learning process. One of the most helpful analyses of the impact of emotions on learning is Goleman's (1995) *Emotional Intelligences.* Based on a careful study of how the brain works and how our minds have evolved, Goleman described how emotions play a "central role the human psyche:"

> Our emotions guide us in facing predicaments and tasks too important to leave to the intellect alone—danger, painful loss,

persisting toward a goal despite frustrations, bonding with a mate, building a family. Each emotion offers a distinctive readiness to act; each points us in a direction that has worked well to handle the recurring challenges of human life. (p. 4)

Connections among emotions and thoughts are especially powerful during early adolescence. In their analysis of emotional development, McDevitt and Ormrod (2007) noted that one of the major accomplishments of childhood is learning to reflect on emotions (p. 420). As children interact with other people they learn to connect words with emotions. They soon realize that people have different emotional responses to shared events. Later, they begin to understand that the expressions people display do not always reflect their true feelings. With this insight, they often begin to try to mask their own emotions. Connections among thoughts and feelings enable children to regulate their emotions and develop coping strategies they can employ when they want to exert greater control over their responses.

McDevitt and Ormrod emphasized three major ways that emotional development grows more sophisticated during the transitions to early adolescence. First, young people begin to recognize ambivalence in their own feelings and in others. As they learn to temper emotional responses with reflections about what they mean, they sometimes feel a stronger sense of confusion, wondering how they really feel. Another major development is a greater capacity for empathy. Understanding more about their own feelings allows them to understand better what other people are feeling. These growing capacities for emotional understanding often result in a third significant transition, self-consciousness regarding their feelings. While some students find this heightened awareness empowering, others risk greater vulnerability. Some students experience unhealthy levels of depression and anxiety. As many as five to ten percent of young people suffer major bouts of depression during early adolescence (p. 427).

37

Eighth grade male: A teacher has accused me of something I did not do. If I get in trouble for something I haven't done, I'll go and do something so I'll be in trouble for something I did. I don't like to be in trouble for things I haven't done. But you feel like you need to get back at the teacher somehow for accusing you when you didn't do it.

Interviewer: How would you get back at the teacher?

Student: If you're doing something that really makes them mad, like playing at the window when they tell you to stop, if you're really ticking them off, you feel like you're getting back at the teacher. You should just ignore it, so you don't have to worry about getting in trouble worse. Sometimes you think about "well I'll just go to lunch" if she wants me to stay back from lunch.

Interviewer: How do you think through step by step?

Student: If I've got time, I'll write down what I can do, and what the consequences are. That way I can really think about what might happen if I get up and walk out to lunch. This same situation happened to me last year. I refused to take the punishment. This girl got water all over the table, and the teacher said I did it. I refused to take lunch detention, and I got two days ISS for it. I had all kinds of witnesses that said I didn't do it, but she didn't believe me.

Interviewer: Looking back on that, was it worth it?

Student: It really wasn't worth it because they threatened to get an officer in there, and they moved all my friends into lunch detention with me, and they got mad at me.

Internal and external dynamics fuel emotional development during adolescence. Biological changes that occur during puberty can cause fluctuations in hormones, creating surges of strong feelings. At the same time, most young people experience more difficult social situations as they transition from childhood. For some students on some occasions, hormonal fluctuations and challenging social settings result in dramatic displays of emotion, providing support for the notion that adolescence is a time of "storm and stress." As we have suggested earlier, it is important for us to remember that many other young people experience little drama, and in fact, learn to regulate their emotions successfully during these developmental transitions.

Goleman (1995; 1998) insisted that parents and educators should be more proactive about teaching "emotional intelligence." Essential goals include helping students identify feelings, manage feelings appropriately, motivate themselves, and respond to the feelings of others. In a study that tested Goleman's theory in a school setting, Qualter, Whiteley, Hutchinson, and Pope (2007) examined the extent to which students with high emotional intelligence (EI) coped better with the transition to high school. Results indicated that students with high or average levels of EI cope better with transition in terms of grade point average, self-worth, school attendance, and behavior than pupils with low EI. Researchers also assessed the impact of an intervention program designed to increase the development of EI competencies. Students with low baseline EI scores responded especially well to the intervention program.

 Harmony

Interviewer: How are things going in your math class?

Seventh grade female: At the beginning of the year, I wasn't really doing much. Now, I am doing most of my homework. If my mind wanders, I try to concentrate better. I stop and tell myself to pay attention. I'm not getting in as much trouble as I used to. I guess I am growing up a little bit.

39

Conclusions

In this chapter, we have explored the intertwined connections that characterize thinking. Research on the workings of the human mind helps us understand that intricate interplay of neurological, cognitive, social, and experiential connections that create our thoughts. Related research helps us appreciate some of the ways that emotions shape and reflect this process. Early adolescence is a critical time in the development of the mind. The complexities inherent in thinking about thinking can seem overwhelming in the classroom. Individuals form thoughts in unique ways, depending on what they understand about the concepts, how they interact with others, and the emotional tones of their thoughts as they experience a lesson. As Cross (1999) concluded,

> Almost daily, an alert teacher will have the "concrete experience" of observing a student—or maybe an entire class—having difficulty with a particular learning task. If she is motivated to learn more about that learning problem, she may "reflect" on whether or where she has seen that problem before. She may then connect it to an "abstract concept," which she may have developed from the experience of clustering similar experiences, or perhaps she has seen something in a textbook that will help to identify the problem as belonging to a cluster of similar problems. She will probably "actively experiment" with several different ways to help that student and others to follow. In the best of all possible worlds, teaching is a continuing learning experience in which the learner/teacher is constantly making connections between experience, reflection, experimentation, and evaluation. (pp. 21–22)

Understanding more about the nature of the connections that create thoughts enables teachers to develop classroom climates that nurture accomplishment. To promote harmony in their classrooms, teachers must consider the interactions among the personal, social, moral, physical, sexual, intellectual, and emotional transitions that characterize early adolescence. In the next chapter, we describe some of the ways that successful teachers orchestrate these dynamics.

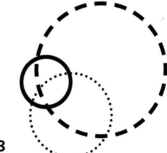

Chapter 3

Physical and Sexual Development

All young adolescents are concerned with their physical and sexual development; for some, their physical development or lack thereof is the dominant, central theme in their lives for a time. While most middle grades teachers know this, some may not make allowances for this "developmental override" when they prepare for their classes; therefore, students may tune into their personal concerns and tune out even the best teachers. Often, directions have to be repeated, explanations restated, and concepts retaught because students "flipped out" of the instructional activities while focusing on a physical or sexual concern.

This kind of developmental override constantly occurs in middle grades classrooms. Educators have to be aware of the root causes of these realities so that they can make appropriate modifications and allowances in their instruction. Since the basic causes are often physical and sexual changes, an overview of the latest research findings in these areas is provided here along with implications for teaching and learning.

Perhaps the best way to begin this profile is to suggest that the reader try to envision some of these changes on a personal level. For example, how would you react to a substantial outbreak of acne or the eruption of a sizable pimple on the end of your nose (a huge "zit" in young adolescent terms)? Though it is not possible for adults to completely get into the mind-set of young adolescents, it is important to try, because the effort alone may lead to better understanding of their needs. Internalizing and reflecting on the common physical and sexual changes is one way of walking in the shoes of young adolescents.

Height and weight

 Reality

Teacher: Something that always amazes me is the variance in size and development that you encounter in a middle school. In one of my eighth grade classes I have a male student who some would mistake as a high school senior. He is over six feet tall and very muscular. He has to shave every morning, and by the end of the day you can already see signs of stubble. In the same class, I have a student who would fit in with the sixth grade students. He is less than five feet tall and probably weighs about 80 pounds soaking wet. When you see them walking down the hall side by side, you would never believe them to be the same age, actually only a two-month age difference.

The average gain in height for a young adolescent is from two to four inches per year, and the average weight gain per year is eight to ten pounds. Over the period of early adolescence from 10 to 15, this averages out to a gain of 10 to 20 inches in height and 40 to 50 pounds (Balk, 1995). These height and weight increases often come in irregular growth spurts and at varying rates of speed (Caskey & Anfara, 2007). If you gained that much weight, you would consider it a serious medical concern; it would likely lead to panic, then to dieting, medication, and exercise and might lead to high blood pressure or heart disease.

42

Interviewer: I can see both of you have done some growing lately. Has there been a time you remember noticing how much you'd grown?

Eighth grade male: I've grown six inches since I started middle school. Just today I saw this girl I always thought was so tall. Today I was almost a head bigger than she was.

Ninth grade male: One month I grew three inches. I knew it because I remembered my height when we were measured at the beginning of the year. Then later we were in the gym and being measured for the scoliosis testing. I saw I measured 5'6". I asked when was the date of the last time I was measured. She said a month ago. I told my Mom because I worried that something might be wrong since it was so fast. Mom said, "Well you're in your big growth spurt. That's normal for a boy your age." That made me feel okay.

In a sense, any averages cited are misleading. They may convey a good overview but ignore the tremendous variations that exist among young adolescents. In the case of physical development, the differences among young adolescents probably pose more of a problem than the substantial height and weight gains that are typical for 10- to 15-year-olds. For example, it is possible for a male student to be 5'5" tall and weigh 115 pounds in the sixth grade and have little or no change occur in height or weight through the seventh, eighth, and even ninth grades. At the same time, another male sixth grader may be 5'9" and weigh 145 pounds and increase in height and weight by the ninth grade to 6'1" and 180 pounds. It is also likely that many girls will be taller than the

Diversity, is characteristic of young adolescents—and is very apparent among these five seventh graders.

43

boy who is 5'5", further compounding the problems of the smaller male. These realities have implications for the classroom.

Our reaction to weight gain by young adolescents is—no problem; this is happening in the way it should. We also assume that middle grades students understand that their weight gain is natural—but many do not. They worry about these changes and believe that something is wrong with them. Research and our own observations confirm the reality that young adolescents continually compare themselves to others (Mack, Strong, Kowalski, & Crocker, 2007). If they are bigger or smaller, shorter or taller than what they perceive to be the norm, young adolescents tend to think that there is something wrong with them. If they deviate from the norm, then they think that they are abnormal. Middle grades students spend a lot of time worrying about their physical differences—at home and at school during classes. What we must understand as educators is that ongoing physical changes influence adolescents' self-esteem, social support network, the amount of teasing by peers, and perceptions of family and friends, thus having a significant impact on their body image and eating-related attitudes (Ata, Ludden, & Lally, 2007; Xiaojia, Elder, Regenrus, & Cox, 2001; Jones & Crawford, 2006; Whetstone, Morrissey, & Cummings, 2007).

Reality

Teacher: I have had some students this year who have lost weight, due to their increased awareness that they were overweight. In fact, I had to call the mother of one student to discuss my concern about her not eating at all during the school day.

Teacher: Among my female students, weight is a major issue for the girls who are significantly larger than their peers, both in height and weight. I even have one student whose mother has put her on a diet (even though in my estimation she is not overweight, just growing faster than her peers). In addition, some female students act the roles they feel are appropriate to their levels of physical development. Girls who are taller and heavier than their peers act tough, while girls who are smaller than average act like much younger children. One small female student, Tanzi, has admitted to me that she acts "like a baby" because her peers (and some adults) treat her like one. With my male students, the problem is reversed. The boys with the most obvious self-esteem issues are the ones who are significantly smaller than their peers. The other children have derogatory nicknames for these small male students; one is "Peanut" and another is "Shrimp." At my school, fights and bullying are omnipresent; smaller boys are very likely to get picked on and beaten up by the larger boys.

Disproportionate growth

Growth in young adolescents, we all know, does not take place evenly (Caskey & Anfara, 2007). That is, certain parts of the body, most notably, the extremities, develop earlier and more rapidly. The young sixth grade male who is 5'9" may wear size 13 shoes that often seem like gunboats to him and everyone else. His feet are simply too big for the rest of his body. The same disproportionate growth is true of hands, since hands also grow more rapidly. This obviously affects movement, and it is common to observe a young adolescent tripping over his or her own feet or reaching across the lunch table for something and spilling milk. The unhappy reality is that they used to be able to walk or reach out without embarrassing themselves, but now these same simple movements often lead to falls, spills, or other undesirable outcomes. When we add to this the more rapid growth of the nose and ears in comparison to the rest of the body, it is not surprising that some students feel like "Bozo the Clown" or "Dumbo the Elephant" and feel that their bodies have betrayed them.

Bone growth and ossification

Adolescence is also a time in which the majority of bone formation occurs (Weaver, 2002). During this period bone growth surpasses muscle growth. That is, the skeletal structure is extending more rapidly than the muscular structure. Since muscles support and protect bones,

45

it is more common for young adolescents to experience bone damage such as fractures or breaks. It is also possible to overextend the capacity of the muscular structure, causing permanent damage to muscle fibers. As an example, many readers may be aware of a young male who was a "star" pitcher when 12, but because he was pushed beyond reasonable limits, lost most of the power in his arm and could not pitch on a high school team at 16. Pushing young adolescents to their "limits" may ultimately lead to lower skill performance in the long run.

During early adolescence, the skeletal structure also begins to harden. Greer and Krebs (2006) reported that, "during the three- to four-year period of increased bone mass acquisition that occurs during adolescence, 40 percent of total lifetime bone mass is accumulated"

Middle school teachers are not averse to selecting the floor over chairs for holding informal conferences.

(p. 579). Recent studies (Cromer & Harel, 2000; Weaver, 2002; Greer & Krebs, 2006) emphasize the importance of calcium intake for adolescents to increase bone density in order to successfully achieve rapid growth. It is safe to assume that adolescents do not consider the short- and long-term effects of reduced calcium intake, such as an increased risk of fractures and osteoporosis. What they do understand, however, is that during this rapid bone growth period they are at times very uncomfortable. In particular, during this time, the tailbone takes on its final form. Three bones fuse together and harden in the posterior area, forming the "mature" tailbone. In the process, students, sitting on hard fiberglass or plastic desks, wiggle and squiggle their way through classes because of this painful, physical transition. The sciatic nerve is closely positioned to the skeletal structure and intensifies student discomfort, thus challenging teachers in their attempts to retain the attention of their students and accept the positions they take.

46

Students regularly complain about uncomfortable furniture and often want taller desks so that "your knees don't hit the top and make the desk rock." Physical discomforts do not enhance the learning process.

Students are also acquiring kneecaps. It is true that all children have knees—but not kneecaps. If the reader doubts this, compare your knee to the knee of a son or daughter who is under ten. Yours could be a bit knobby, perhaps too knobby, and a young child's will have a hard surface but no definite cap. Kneecaps are bestowed (for free) on young adolescents. They do not wake up one morning, look down at their legs and exclaim, "Oh, I've got kneecaps." But kneecaps do develop over a period of months during this stage of life. The cartilage and sinew around the knees coalesce and ossify to form this protective device for this critical joint.

To comprehend the full impact of these processes, the reader might wish to compare the way young adolescents sit and move when given the opportunity to choose where and how to sit as compared to the way they sit in school. If they sit in a chair at home, it is not a hard, wooden one. Actually, many young adolescents lounge on the floor, moving around a lot, and create a wide variety of lotus-like positions using chairs only for their feet. It really should not surprise us that middle level students wiggle and fidget a lot in school. They are so uncomfortable that they need to move their bodies around in a never-ending quest to feel comfortable.

 Harmony

Interviewer: How was your transition from fifth grade to sixth? Did anything surprise you?

Sixth grade male: All we heard in elementary was how strict things would be at the middle school, you know, like you had better be ready to be really serious. I guess I was surprised by our math teacher. He is a really nice guy and he gets us up and moving during his lessons. We have these "cheers" we do— like for the order of operations—silly but we get to move around.

47

Perspiration

Reality

> **Language arts teacher:** You can always tell in which hallway the sixth graders are located. A mixture of body odor, cologne, and deodorant lingers in the air. The kids come back from PE still sweating from playing basketball. Most kids take showers, but the shower doesn't always ensure that deodorant is being used. This may sound strange, but the smell doesn't seem to bother the kids as much as it does the teachers.

Although parents notice that their young children perspire when very active, parents of young adolescents are not always so observant of the effect of increased physical prowess and surging hormones in their children. Sweat and sex glands become very active and emit odors that are not just unpleasant, but offensive. Perspiration may be too polite a term to use; the term "sweat" seems to catch the full implication of the locker room odor that drifts into classrooms with the students. Although most parents supply and encourage their growing youngsters to use deodorant, teachers may have to resort to using circulating fans to blow odors out of classrooms on hot days.

Hormonal changes

The pituitary glands generate increases in hormones. This serves as a catalyst for more rapid growth and also as a controller of glands that determine tissue growth and function. Unfortunately, the control of the other glands such as the adrenal glands is irregular. This irregular control is unfortunate because it leads to the secretion of adrenalin in "huge" quantities when it is not needed at all. For example, as a student dutifully works on 20 square root problems in her seat, she receives an adrenalin secretion that is substantial enough for her to run the length of a football field ten times without stopping. This hormonal secretion is akin to an electrical power surge, and it makes the student squirm and want to move, stretch, and perhaps yell at the top of her lungs. However, she is expected to work quietly on square roots or some other assignment such as dangling participles. Only the most self-disciplined young adolescent can sit quietly at times like these.

Nutrition

Some observers affectionately refer to the stomachs of young adolescents as bottomless pits. This is not quite true. The stomach does become longer, increases in capacity, and the typical middle school student often craves food. This is the result of the draining off of nutrients into the rapid growth of body organs. At times, young adolescents are so hungry that "it hurts." The food has been used up, and they need to replenish their bodies. They will sneak bites off a candy bar fully aware that such is prohibited. And understanding middle school teachers often overlook such an occurrence.

Reality

> **Seventh grade female:** I do not want to get fat so I try not to eat everything on the plate, but I am so hungry that I always do. See, I want to be a cheerleader, and you can't be fat if you are a cheerleader cause they wear short skirts, and everyone could tell that you were too fat. Next year I am not going to eat all my pizza and maybe get salad instead of ice cream.

To compensate for this, students often overload their stomachs by gorging themselves, which leads to digestive disturbances. This condition is exacerbated by the peculiar eating tendencies of young adolescents. If left unguided, many may eat only fried food, candy, rich desserts, and drink only carbonated beverages. The National Center for Chronic Disease Prevention and Health Promotion (2006) reported the following:

> Unfortunately, many young people in the United States make poor eating choices that put them at risk for health and social problems.

- Having breakfast can affect children's intellectual performance.

- Poor eating habits and inactivity are the root causes of overweight and obesity. The prevalence of overweight among children ages 6 to 11 has more than doubled in the past 20 years, going from seven percent in 1980 to 18.8 percent in 2004. Overweight among youth ages 12 to 19 has tripled in the same time period, going from five percent to 17.4 percent.
- Overweight children have a higher rate of low self-esteem, type 2 diabetes, sleep apnea, bone and joint problems, and gall bladder disease.
- As many as seven to eight percent of females in the United States suffer from anorexia nervosa or bulimia nervosa in their lifetime.
- Many children and adolescents have a diet too low in fruit and vegetables and too high in saturated fat.
- Eighty-five percent of adolescent females do not consume enough calcium.
- A large number of high school students use unhealthy methods to lose or maintain weight. A nationwide survey found that during the 30 days preceding the survey 12.3 percent of high school students went without eating for 24 hours or more; 4.5 percent had vomited or taken laxatives; and 6.3 percent had taken diet pills, powders, or liquids without a doctor's advice.

Teachers often observe two patterns in relation to student nutrition. First, a number of students come to school in the morning without ever eating breakfast, appear lethargic from lack of sleep or nutrition, and have a limited attention span. They then return from lunch often on a brief "sugar high." For many of these students the last period is a battle to stay awake. The second pattern is evident among those students who eat a well-balanced breakfast and lunch. These students seem to spend more time on task and are usually more active in the instructional phase of the lesson. Teachers often then have to adjust and revise class schedules around student nutritional habits and conditions. The increase in schools that provide free or minimal cost breakfast has alleviated this problem to a certain extent. In addition, a number of teachers are addressing eating concerns as parts of thematic curriculum units. When we combine the impact of poor nutrition habits with the irregular secretions of hormones and the overproduction of sweat glands, acne and other skin defects are often the result. A pimple on the end of one's nose is rarely a laughing matter. Pimples all over the face of a young adolescent can be tragic. Since young adolescents are more self-conscious about their appearance than any other age group, their reaction to pimples is similar to their reaction to the bubonic plague. Though worse things could occur, most middle school students with acne think the worse has already occurred.

 Reality

Ninth grade male: Most of all I worry about my complexion. It is always breaking out. My mom takes me to a dermatologist and sometimes it is better than others, but it is a real problem most of the time. The dermatologist told me I might have this problem until I am 21. I don't even want to think about it. I also wanted to wear braces because all my friends were wearing them. I guess that sounds silly to a grown-up.

Hair

A quick Internet search using the words "middle school" and "hair" reveals scores of Web sites dedicated to discussing this topic (blogs) and giving free or paid advice via product endorsements. In short, hair, and the concept of hairstyles are near or at the top of issues related to middle school image. Hairstyle can impact status within an identity group or quickly send someone into middle school social exile. When we look back at Arth's (1992) survey of a number of middle school students in different settings soliciting their reactions to themselves and their school experiences, it appears that the survey could have been taken yesterday. When the students were asked, "What one thing would you change about yourself?" his findings indicated that the overwhelming majority would change their hair. It was too long, too short, too curly, too straight, too full, etc.—but it was consistently unacceptable as it is. This may explain why middle school students are continually fiddling with their hair. It often does not feel right, and since it is so readily visible, hair has to be worked on to make it look better—whatever better is. The authors truly believe that this one aspect of adolescence will probably never change.

 Reality

Teacher: When I asked Ashley why she was late, she said she missed the bus because her hair was being "really stupid and ugly."' I noticed that locker time for Ashley is a very big part of her day. When she opens her locker, I see a very organized display of "necessary" beauty products (such as hair spray and goo; various shades of lip gloss; nail polish and remover; cotton balls, and cotton swabs), a large mirror on the inside door, numerous bright stickers of butterflies, etc. adorning the locker's interior, and tear-out photos of current heartthrobs.

Puberty

As children move into early adolescence, a series of sexual changes begin to occur that are of the utmost interest to them. The major change is that the primary sex hormones, estrogen and testosterone, are produced by two stimulating hormones—the follicle stimulating hormone (FSH) and the luteinizing hormone (LH). When the levels of these two stimulating hormones increase, an individual's gonads (primary sex glands—the ovaries and testes) begin to mature (Neinstein, 2004). There is tremendous variation as to when these changes begin to occur and how rapidly they take place. These differences in sexual development lead to a great deal of concern and anxiety.

As stated previously, because of the compelling tendency to compare self to others, young adolescents, especially females, can inevitably develop negative feelings about their bodies (O'Dea & Abraham, 1999; Ata, Ludden, & Lally, 2007; Xiaojia, Elder, Regenrus, & Cox, 2001; Jones & Crawford, 2006; Whetstone, Morrissey, & Cummings, 2007).

52

If they use their parents as models of what they should be, they judge themselves to be less endowed (at least, in most cases). If they observe the differences between themselves and older brothers or sisters, they also "lose." Since they typically compare themselves to their peers, they also view themselves as less desirable. If they are smaller in breast development or penis development, they feel less adequate. If they are taller or bigger, they tend to feel self-conscious because they also deviate from the norm. Being bigger usually poses less of a problem than being smaller. The main point is, when young adolescents compare themselves to others they inevitably lose. A specific illustration may help.

One of our colleagues often recalled an incident with "Mike the Magnificent" from his own middle years. Mike was a young male, middle level in chronological age, but far beyond others in sexual development. He was very muscular, very hairy, very sizable, and proud of himself. During group showers at school, most students would "skulk" around keeping our meager selves covered with towels. Not Mike. Mike would strut around without cover or inhibition very proud of his accouterments. This certainly did not help others come to terms with their less endowed bodies. To this day, this memory probably remains emblazoned in their minds as an example of what most would never become.

It is assumed that for every Mike, there is a "Barbie," a female counterpart. If this is the case, it is not surprising that young adolescents, very anxious about their sexual development, may feel rather intimidated by these models. It is also not surprising that some students refuse to dress out so that they can avoid being embarrassed by their "allegedly" underdeveloped bodies. Because our society places such a heavy emphasis on this area and reinforces perfection in sexual appearance through the media, young people suffer for no good reason. They judge themselves to be inadequate because they must compare— and they are exposed to sexual role models that are close to perfection.

Interviewer: What do you like least about your school?

Ninth grade male, age 13: I don't like PE. I guess I especially don't like the showers. None of the kids shower here. I haven't seen one kid take a shower since I've been here. They have nice showers in the gym, but no one uses them. Luckily I have PE 7th period, and if I'm all hot and sweaty, I can shower when I get home.

Ninth grade male, age 14: I don't like the showers in PE. No one uses the showers. The teachers don't make us shower. They know we don't like it. Some of the guys shower in their underwear. Can you imagine sitting around all day in wet clothes? It's awful. I tried this, but now I don't shower at school.

The reality is that a wide range in sexual development exists, and variations should be accepted as normal. We should provide the factual data on this to our students. It might be one of the more helpful contributions we could make to young adolescents. Assuming such data would be very helpful, one overview of the variations in sexual development is provided here followed by a commentary on some of the common sexual concerns that middle level students experience.

The events of puberty in girls and boys

Children's Hospital Boston (2007) reported that puberty changes occur in females between the ages of 8 and 13 years old and for males between 9.5 and 14 years old. For females:

- First pubertal change: breast development.
- Pubic hair development: shortly after breast development.
- Hair under the arms: 12 years of age.
- Menstrual periods: 10 to 16.5 years of age.

For males:
- First pubertal change: enlargement of the testicles.
- Penis enlargement: begins approximately one year after the testicles begin enlarging.
- Appearance of pubic hair: 13.5 years of age.
- Hair under the arms, on the face, voice change, and acne: 15 years of age.
- Nocturnal emissions (or wet dreams): 14 years of age.

It is important to note that these ages are central tendencies in a wide age range. Half have become involved in the event by the average age while half have not. These ranges are extensive and are important to recognize. Young adolescent girls and boys should be given these basic facts about the ranges for the events of puberty and facts about their sexual development. Hockenberry-Eaton and Richman's (1996) study on adolescent knowledge of sexual development revealed that adolescents were unable to adequately define most of the basic sexual development terms. This lack of knowledge makes educators, rather than television shows or music videos, the ones who ought to provide factual information.

 Reality

Interviewer: When sex education is taught, are boys and girls separated?

Eighth grade male: Well, we were separated in the sixth grade, but not in the seventh grade. Everyone was together for the same stuff.

Interviewer: Did anyone get embarrassed? Did you feel uncomfortable about asking questions?

Student: Yeah, most of the kids did get really embarrassed about all of the stuff with guys and the girls in the same class. We really didn't want to ask a lot of questions.

One assurance that youth in the middle grades need to have is that everything will take place in its own time. Nature keeps its own biological clock, and the timing, whether one likes it or not, cannot be changed. Sexual development will occur, and no one needs to feel bad if his or her development does not occur at the rate or time that he or she wants it to occur; it is beyond a person's control. In the same way, young adolescents who are bigger or smaller in terms of sexual features are not better—they have just developed that way. This last statement needs to be said as convincingly and as often as possible.

Discord

Eighth grade female: I hate PE because it is really boring. We just learn the rules to the games but never get much time to play. We have to dress out in PE and that is kind of embarrassing. Our teacher is mean and she calls you by your last name.

It is also important to help these young people understand a few other facts about some of these events. For example, girls may begin to menstruate, but their periods may be very irregular. It may be two years before a regular adult cycle is established because the ovaries may not release an egg each month. Boys may be interested in knowing that the enlargement of the testes is almost always the first event of puberty for them, not the appearance of pubic hair as is commonly thought.

Young adolescents also worry because their bodies behave in a peculiar manner at times. For some boys, an erection may occur at a most undesirable time (e.g. in math or language arts class) for no apparent reason. Girls may be sexually stimulated and also embarrassed in a similar manner and time. Young males and females need to know that these episodes may happen to some and not to others, but that they needn't be overly concerned.

Eighth grade female: I think there should be more sex education. We study sex, but I think it should be stressed more. Sometimes when we're studying it, people will laugh. I think it should be offered through science. Health is considered more of a fun thing because it's mixed in with gym. If it were offered in science maybe people wouldn't laugh so much because they'd be getting a more serious grade.

Interviewer: That's a good idea. Are the boys and girls in the same class?

Student: Sometimes. We didn't discuss sex together, but we saw some of the films together about when a girl grows up and when a boy grows up. We studied the adolescent changes together.

Interviewer: What did they tell you about the adolescent changes?

Student: It was okay, but boys are so silly. They had to laugh at everything. They want to see the girl's film with the girls, but they didn't want to see the boy's film with the girls.

Interviewer: Do you think they were embarrassed?

Student: They were being silly!

Sexual activity and pregnancy

A number of research studies verify the trend over the last several decades toward increased sexual activity at a younger age. The Center for Disease Control Youth Risk Behavior Survey (2007) reported that 49.8 percent of the male youths and 45.9 percent of the females in this country will have had sexual intercourse prior to leaving high school. Additionally, the percentage of students who have had intercourse for the first time before the age of 13 years increased from 2001 (6.6%) to 2007 (7.1%). Interestingly, over 89 percent of students have been taught about AIDS and HIV infection, yet only 61.5 percent of students who are currently sexually active report that either they or their partner used a condom the last time they had sexual intercourse. The Federal Interagency Forum on Child and Family Statistics (2008) report *America's Children in Brief: Key National Indicators of Well-Being* shows that teen pregnancy rates have increased from 21 births per 1000 in 2005 to 22 births per 1000 in 2006. This research indicates that adolescents have increasingly become involved in more casual, less committed sexual activity. With the ongoing reality of teenage pregnancy, HIV, and other sexually transmitted diseases, this is a serious problem that must be addressed. Helping young males and females to be more sexually aware and responsible is a necessity at the middle level.

Sexual preference

It is clear that many young adolescents struggle with their sex role identity. They are also uncertain about what is normal. For example, same sex friendship is the dominant pattern for this age group, but it generates concern for some young people. They may think that their preference for being friends with members of the same sex is abnormal. In reality, it is perfectly appropriate.

Reality

Teacher: Some students are sexually mature, while others have not even entered puberty. Among my female students, there is a great deal of anxiety regarding menstruation, both for those who have begun menstruation already and for those who have not. Sexual activity is also an important issue for my students. Many students at my school are already engaging in sexual activity. I have even had two students become pregnant this year—one student elected to have an abortion, while the other gave birth last month. Many students are clearly having sex, even at surprisingly young ages. Finally, sexual orientation is an issue for some of my students. At my school, students regularly refer to homosexuality in a derogatory way, creating a hostile environment for students who are gay, bisexual, or questioning.

Conclusion

As young adolescents make their way through numerous physical and sexual developmental changes, they believe that someone is always watching them or that they are always on stage. In 1967, David Elkind first referred to this myth as the "imaginary audience." The result of this egotism is that adolescents often form exaggerated beliefs about their own uniqueness because they do not distinguish their thoughts and feelings from what others think and feel (Balk, 1995). While it may be obvious to adults that young adolescents are not always being observed, it is almost impossible to convince these young people of this. Perhaps this is why privacy at home in one's own room or some other place becomes so important. The young adolescent can squirrel away out of sight, turn the music up (way up, perhaps to be sure that no one can hear his or her thoughts), close the door, and eliminate the imaginary audience for a little while. Because it is stressful living on stage day after day, this is a way for a young person to escape from the pressure.

Because young adolescents think they are always being watched, they also engage in another peculiar activity that we call "mirror checking." It seems as though middle level students are drawn to mirrors like metal to magnets and will check themselves out in any mirror available as often as they can. We contend that young adolescents do mirror checks every 15 minutes or so to see what else has changed since the last time they looked. Has a new freckle surfaced or is a new pimple patch developing? They need to know how they look at all times in case they run into, sometimes literally, anyone they know, especially a member of the opposite sex.

All of these uneven changes may also lead to a rather negative view of "self." The internal message that must run through the minds of many middle level students at an unconscious level goes something like this: "My body has betrayed me. I'm ugly and clumsy. I've got zits and I can't control myself. I'm bigger than or smaller than everyone else. No one has problems as big as mine and no one could possibly understand me." This unhappy message is a common tune ending on a sour note. Typical adolescents believe that their stories are so unique and their troubles so great and different that no one, especially adults, can appreciate their needs, interests, or concerns. This myth called "egocentrism" places the middle level student in a world that is lonely and frightening. Educators who keep these physical changes in mind and understand this myth and its impact will be much more effective.

Finally, television, media, cinema, and music have all conveyed a series of "misconceptions" to young adolescents about their own sexuality. A great deal of confusion exists in their minds about the events of puberty. Yet, these events play a dominant role in the way young adolescents think, feel, and behave. They deserve to be properly informed. Educators need to debunk myths and provide a solid base of factual information. Teachers also need to be available to listen to and provide guidance to middle level students in regard to what is happening or not happening in the area of sexual development and what to say and do in regard to relating to members of the opposite sex. This kind of assistance can provide invaluable service to our young adolescents as they struggle to understand their own sexuality. Responding to students in supportive ways is especially important to nurturing their social, personal, and moral development—issues we explore in the chapter that follows.

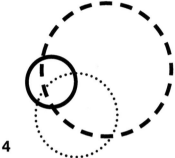

Chapter 4

Social, Personal, and Moral Development

Successful middle level teachers create classroom environments that respond to the varied needs of their students. Such environments have to start with supportive and affirmative relationships with caring teachers that enable young adolescents to develop personal and academic momentum. This process depends on trust. Students need to trust their teachers, classmates, and indeed, themselves. In this chapter we will examine the social, personal, and moral aspects of development that make these dynamics so important.

Perhaps the most important developmental accomplishment of early adolescence is a stronger sense of identity. As they grow toward adulthood, children naturally begin to think more deeply about themselves—who they are and how they best relate to those around them. They define themselves, to a large extent, by how "significant others" treat them. And next to parents, middle level teachers are commonly the prime significant others. Friends and other family members, of course, also play key roles. Identity formation is thus inextricably interwoven with social, personal, and moral development.

 Reality

Anthony is not your typical eighth grade student. He will turn 16 years old in a few months. When he is among a group of classmates he may be mistaken for the teacher or another adult in the school. The snake tattoos on both arms accentuate the muscular forearms that have been developed by doing manual labor with his father for several years. His thin mustache reinforces his "man among the boys" attitude. As we begin to speak before school one morning, I'm reminded that last night's social studies homework is far from the top of his priority list. He already has a two-year-old daughter and thinks his girlfriend may be pregnant again. His parents are threatening to kick him out of the house if he doesn't straighten up his act. One morning some time ago, Mark spoke with Anthony in the commons area of his school while several hundred students waited for school to start. Mark asked Anthony to share his perceptions of his peers. Listening to his comments, Anthony sounded more like a graduate student conducting research than an at-risk student whose days in school were likely numbered.

Mr. L.: Anthony, tell me about some of the different groups of kids who are here in the commons area.

Anthony: No problem. (He begins to move through the crowd of students who part his path as quickly as they see him approaching) Over there you got the "Home Boys." They think they are bad and some of them do drugs—or say they do. They try to pretend they're gang members and always get in trouble in school. That group next to them is the "Wannabe Home Boys" who try to hang out with the "homeys" but aren't allowed to. Sometimes some of the "homeys" make the "wannabes" do stupid stuff just so they can watch them get in trouble.

62

Mr. L.: How do you become a "Home Boy"?

Anthony: You got to live in their neighborhood. (He waves to several of the Homey's as we walk by. A couple of them are looking at Tony—the name they use for Anthony—trying to figure why he is walking around with a teacher. No one questions him openly.) Over there you got the "Preppies." They are the rich kids who live in big houses and always are talking about spending money and going on trips. They're nothing but snobs. Most of those girls won't even talk to me. Look at the clothes they wear. I would never buy my clothes from those stupid stores. (The girls in the group pay no attention to Tony as he walks by. The boys in the group deliberately try to avoid Tony's intimidating glare.)

Mr. L: Anthony, how come this group of "Preppies" isn't with the other group?

Anthony: They ain't "preppies." They're "wannabes." You can always tell a wannabe preppie because they don't wear the same label clothing as the preppies. They can't afford it. Some of them come from the same trailer park as me. (Anthony refuses to recognize a couple of attempts by students in the group to say hello.)

Anthony: One thing we got at this school Mr. L. is "nerds." We got all kinds of "nerds." Look over there. Those are the "smart nerds." They get As on everything they do. They aren't in my classes. They get put in the classes for smart kids. Then you've got your weird nerds. They just stick by themselves and act all stupid.

Anthony finishes his tour by providing descriptions of the remaining peer groups (burnouts, jocks, and loners).

Identity formation during early adolescence

This timeless vignette, with slight changes in the details or terms, could describe adolescents in just about any period of history. The names

63

and number of groups may change but the central theme remains—adolescents are on a quest to fit into a peer group while at the same time struggling to define themselves. They need to answer the questions "Who am I?" and "Where do I fit in?" Although the inner workings of identity development may be more complex than Anthony's biased descriptions of peer groups, this eighth grader has an implicit understanding of how stressful and traumatic group relationships can be for identity formation.

Observers of middle school students regularly note that young adolescents seem to hold a number of identities concurrently. Depending on the context and the value of the relationship, adolescents seem quite proficient in being able to adapt. Teachers often complain that parents will tell them that their child is an "angel" at home. This is the same child who can be disrespectful in class and sometimes treats peers with disdain. Trying on different identities may be part of their quest to define themselves, or as someone once phrased it, "trying on many masks until they find the face that fits."

Suggesting that "identity is the central theme of adolescence," Josselson (1994) defined identity as the adolescent's efforts to claim membership in the social world, to stand for something, to be known for who one is. This search consists of both process and product. Identity acts as "an unfolding bridge" linking individual and society, childhood and adulthood. Finkenauer, Engels, Meeus, and Oosterwegal (2002) stated that, "identity represents the aspect of self that is accessible and salient in a particular context, that interacts in the environment, and to which the person is committed" (p.28).

Within these general trends of identity formation, young adolescents experience a wide range of differences. Interactions among internal development and external situations guarantee that each person forms a sense of identity that is unique for that person. Answers to the questions "Who am I?" and "Where do I fit in?" vary greatly depending on the ways that individuals respond to different situations and the ways that other people respond to them.

Gender is certainly a factor in identity formation. As children, students develop clear "gender schemas," self-constructed understandings of "what males are like" and "what females are like" (McDevitt & Ormrod, 2007, p. 451). As children become young adolescents, these gender schemas grow more sophisticated. Middle school students often take greater interest in activities that reflect their idealized views of masculinity or femininity. Boys may devote more time and energy learning about sports, for example, even if they do not really enjoy participating. McDevitt and Ormrod report a number of studies that document trends in gender differences related to identity. In general, middle school boys tend to overestimate their abilities to solve problems, while girls underestimate theirs; girls consider themselves better behaved and more socially considerate; girls tend to judge their appearances more harshly than do boys (p. 452). In spite of intensive efforts to encourage girls to take greater interest in math and science, boys continue to rate their abilities higher in these areas than do girls (Herbert, Stipek, & Miles, 2003). As McDevitt and Ormrod reported from personal experience, some young women think through these "sex role stereotypes" when they get to high school or college and do very well in math and science (p. 451).

In recent years, researchers have learned more about ethnicity as another factor in identity development. Brown and Leamen (2007) presented a powerful summary of studies documenting ways that, in addition to the typical issues of identity development, students of color often face additional challenges. As they become more socially aware, many students experience racism and prejudice more intensively and internalize the power of ethnic differences.

Messages that students of color receive about their identity may originate via institutions like schools through tracking students by ability or busing students to schools in other neighborhoods. Young adolescents are likely to identify racism through social events that occur, such as reactions by teachers or parents to interracial dating or racist remarks from other students. Media images, both positive and negative, may have the greatest influence on ethnically diverse young adolescents' perceptions about others' attitudes concerning them. (p. 223)

In some cases, these negative experiences contribute to what Ogbu (1991) and others have described as "oppositional identity," the belief that oppression by the majority culture is so strong that one can preserve his or her own identity only by acting in opposition. Brown and Leamen (2007) encourage teachers to promote more positive perceptions of ethnic identity by understanding cultural responsiveness, recognizing and honoring students' ethnicity, and creating curricular connections to issues of ethnic identity.

These studies underscore the importance of understanding factors related to identity formation. For the past 40 years, one of the most influential theories has been Erikson's (1968) stages model of identity development. Three of the eight stages he identified are central to the transition from childhood toward adulthood:

- Industry versus inferiority (elementary school years): The child must deal with learning new skills or risk a sense of inferiority, failure, and incompetence.
- Identity versus role confusion (adolescence): The adolescent must achieve identity in social, biological, and cultural areas.
- Intimacy versus isolation (young adulthood): The young adult attempts to establish positive intimate relationships or face the possibility of isolation and becoming ostracized. (McDevitt & Ormrod, 2007, p. 405)

In the decades since Erikson published his work, a number of researchers have explored these dynamics to better understand how young people adapt to the stresses, demands, and consequences of our changing society.

Roesser, Eccles, and Sameroff (2000) suggested an integrative perspective on "psychosocial identity" that links the development of young adolescents' views of who they are with the levels of support offered them by their families, schools, and communities.

66

His (Erikson's) 1968 treatise on adolescent identity was meant to draw attention to his contention that an adolescent's ability to organize the significant changes they experience during these years into a coherent and positive psychosocial identity was not simply a personal project but rather a collective and intergenerational responsibility of the adolescent and his or her parents, teachers, and community members. (p. 444)

Analysis of data from a longitudinal study of almost 1500 young adolescents and their families shows that three essential aspects of adolescents' lives shape their views of themselves, their social well-being, and their success in school: 1) how well their experiences support a sense of competence; 2) how well their experiences support a sense of autonomy; and 3) the quality of their relationships with peers and adults (Roesser, Eccles, & Sameroff, 2000).

Subsequent studies have affirmed the power of these three essential dynamics—competence, autonomy, and social interactions (Moneta, Schneider & Csikszentmihalyi, 2001; Dusek & McIntyre, 2003). Consequently, we have organized our analysis of social, personal, and moral development using these three themes. Young adolescents "negotiate" their views of themselves—how competent

Young adolescents often use the inside of their lockers to affirm an identity.

they can be, how independent they can be, how well they can get along with others—in their interactions with other people. Over time, in the "give and take" of these interactions, they form a stronger sense of identity or reinforce beliefs of inadequacy.

Negotiating issues of competence

In response to the turbulent changes they experience in their physical and intellectual development, young adolescents experience dramatic changes in self-concept. More than anything else, young adolescents need to develop views of themselves as valuable, able, and responsible people within an inviting, supportive, and safe environment (Purkey & Strahan, 1986; L'Esperance, Strahan, Farrington & Anderson, 2003; Payne, 2005). As we noted in Chapter 2, it is during this developmental period that intellectual changes make it possible for students to think about thinking. The most powerful implication of this ability is a newfound capacity for introspection. For the first time in their lives, young adolescents can think about who they are in functional ways. Everyone they meet affects everything they do and their views of themselves. The key to flourishing through the ongoing expectation of adolescence is having an understanding of one's own self-confidence and having the power to adapt to strengthen it within each context (Cichucki, 2007).

Self-concept first emerges as a "global" construct. That is, students see themselves as able or unable, responsible or irresponsible, valuable, or all but worthless. It is only in later adolescence that their views of themselves begin to differentiate to include specific dimensions of strength and weakness.

 Reality

Eighth grade female: I worry about getting an F on a test or forgetting an answer when the teacher calls on me. At the beginning of the year, I always worry about having friends and if I will have anyone to sit with on the bus and at lunch. Another thing I worry about is having a boyfriend. My sister is real pretty and boys call her on the phone all the time. Boys don't like me 'cause I'm not tall. If a boy says something to me, I never have anything to say back until he leaves and then it is too late. Sometimes I wish I were more like my sister 'cause everyone likes her and she can always think of things to say.

A useful analogy for perceptions of competence is the "Poker Chip Theory" suggested by Canfield and Wells (1976). The authors suggested that each student enters each class with a self-concept that is like a stack of chips. Some have had successful experiences in the past and enter with big stacks of chips. Others have been less successful and enter with small stacks. As in a poker game, the students with the larger stacks can afford to take chances and try new experiences. Those students who feel they have only a few chips left are not likely to take risks unless they can see a "sure thing." The ways in which teachers respond to students help them increase or decrease their stacks of chips.

One of the most powerful influences on perceptions of competence is comparison of self to others. Unfortunately, such comparisons often result in feelings of inadequacy, as discussed in the previous chapter. The media make such comparison unavoidable. Television shows and videos project "perfect" and not so perfect role models into our homes and onto our computer screens (Van Hoose, 1983; Giroux, 1996; Ravitch & Veteritti, 2006). Manning's (2007) study of adolescent self-esteem showed how the strength of social comparison grows stronger as children grow older.

> Students frequently display a decline in self-concept during later elementary grades and into the transition to the middle level. This decrease represents an adaptive reaction to the overly positive self-perceptions that are characteristic of childhood. Young children tend to overestimate their competence because they lack the cognitive maturity to critically evaluate their abilities and to integrate information from multiple sources. (pp. 37-38)

Young adolescents who compare themselves to others and see themselves coming up short may begin to believe that they are inadequate. They may then develop patterns of behavior to match perceived inadequacies. These coping behaviors are attempts at compensating for "flaws" or denying that "flaws" exist in themselves. One young person may become a fierce competitor in a sport. Another may become a perfectionist in academics. A third may direct all energies toward being more popular. Some middle level students attempt to deny their inadequacies by not speaking out in class (so that they cannot be told they are wrong) or by becoming a physical bully (so that no one can overtly reject them socially). In more destructive forms, a young adolescent may resort to drugs, avoid health care, or engage in other risk-taking behaviors to avoid dealing with a painful reality (Wyatt & Peterson, 2005; Smith & Donnerstein, 2006; Aalsma, Lapsley, & Flannery, 2006; Johnson & Malow-Iroff, 2008).

To illustrate some of the ways that young adolescents express perceptions of competence, the authors asked several eighth grade students to define the term "popular" and write a personal reflection related to how they view themselves in relation to their own definition. The range of responses reveals the impact this concept has on identity formation.

> Popular students are smart, nice, and outgoing. They are people that others look up to. Popular people aren't scared to get up and talk in front of a class because they know what to say or do. People will listen and laugh just because they know who you are. Popular people play sports and are funny. They walk around in big groups and have fun.

> I would consider myself popular because I play every sport in the school. Everyone is my friend and I was voted "King of the School" and "Strongest Person in the School." I also date the most popular girl in the school. Everyone listens when I talk and laughs when I tell a joke. I guess you could say that I fill in all the categories of a very popular person.

> Popular students at this school would be first categorized by their family's financial status and then by the clothes they wear. An unpopular student is someone who is poor, not at all attractive, or doesn't dress the right way. I would consider myself in the middle. I used to be really unpopular, but now I've moved up. I am friends with almost everyone. I guess I'm popular because I'm nice… and most girls are popular with the guys because of their looks. I mean, I'm not trying to be snobby or anything, but I'm not all that ugly.

To be popular you have to have name brand clothes like: Abercrombie™, Gap™, Polo™, and American Eagle™, just to name a few. You have to have a lot of friends. An unpopular person doesn't wear name brand clothes. They might be considered a dork or a geek. I do consider myself popular. I'm sorry to say it, but sometimes the people I hang out with can be mean to the unpopular people. At times I wish I wasn't popular. It would be a lot easier not to care what people think about me and not to worry if my friends are gonna like my new outfit.

Being popular means that everyone likes you and you are well known. Being unpopular means that hardly anyone likes you other than your family. If you are unpopular you are usually made fun of. I would consider myself unpopular because I'm disliked and made fun of. Actually, I'm made fun of daily. And to tell you the truth it gets aggravating.

I think a popular person is someone who wears stylish clothes and has a lot of friends. A popular person does good in school, is loud, and plays sports or some other activity after school. A popular person also has nice hair and teeth and takes a shower every day. No, I don't think I'm popular. I get picked on because I'm not stylish or athletic. But they don't understand that everyone can't afford spending $100 on shoes or a shirt. I get a pair of pants for $7.50 and shoes for $10 that are very good. No my teeth aren't right but I do take showers, brush my teeth, and use deodorant.

A popular person is a student who is nice, funny, cute or good looking. I think an unpopular person is someone who is like me. I am ugly, stupid, and failing eighth grade. So no, I have to say, I'm not popular.

The differences among these eighth graders in their views of themselves and their classmates underscore the variability of self-perceptions.

Across the middle grades, many young people learn to see themselves as competent persons. They internalize a sense of self-worth. Experiences with success, in and out of school, provide a reservoir of skill and will. Faced with challenging tasks, they draw confidence from previous accomplishments, believe that they can be successful, and invest energy in their efforts. Other students are not so fortunate. Many negative experiences create doubts about themselves and they fare poorly in self-comparisons.

Negotiating issues of autonomy

Because young adolescents are in a transitional stage; they vacillate in their social and moral behaviors from being childlike to being more like adults. In addition to wanting to feel more self-worth, they seek a stronger sense of autonomy; that is, they want to do things independently. The Larson, Richards, Meneta, and Duckett (1996) study of adolescents' daily interactions with their families concluded that the percentage of students who spent an average of 35 percent of their day with family as fifth graders decreases to 14 percent as eighth graders. Barnes, Hoffman, Welte, Farrell, and Dintcheff (2007) studied the time use and risk-taking behaviors of 15- to 18-year-old adolescents and reported that participants spent about 10 hours per week in family related activities versus 23 hours per week with peers. These estimates indicate that across the middle level years, most youth spend increasing amounts of time with peers and encounter a variety of experiences outside the family.

This trend toward autonomy also resonates throughout the school day and is evident in the direct attention given to hearing and honoring student voice that is so much a part of the middle school concept.

At times, adolescents may want to be completely independent and think that they can undertake a task and complete it rather easily. For example, a teacher can explain the nature and use of adverbs and the students clearly see that it is easy for the teacher so it will be easy for them. They have no questions, and they can apply the concepts just taught. Then, when asked to work on a few simple exercises, they storm the teacher for guidance. They thought they knew and understood the concepts very well but found that they just could not do what was expected. They shift, in a heartbeat, from independent to dependent.

 Harmony

Thirteen-year-old male: Some of the teachers are great. Notice I said SOME. I think the best teachers let you talk with each other sometimes, maybe when we are working in groups. These teachers also talk with us in class. Sometimes they talk to us about things that are not in our lessons, and sometimes they talk with us about the lessons. You can talk about different things other than school subjects. I feel relaxed with these teachers. We trust each other. They seem to trust us, and we trust them back. If you think they graded your paper wrong, they will give you a chance to come up and talk to them about it and we are not afraid of them.

The development of moral reasoning is clearly connected to the adolescent quest for independence. Young adolescents move from seeing moral dilemmas as external to themselves to looking at right and wrong in clearly defined terms. As their intellectual and social development continues, they soon find themselves rebelling against or testing the structures of school and home. Smetana and Turiel (2003) suggested that "adolescents are not consistently principled, moral thinkers, as some have claimed, nor are they morally confused and selfish individualists, as others have asserted. Adolescents make autonomous moral judgments in some situations and focus on personal goals in others" (p. 263). Friends and social networks also influence the construction of boundaries between legitimate parental and personal authority. Daddis' (2008) concluded,

> Same-age friends may influence each other by acting as guides when adolescents look to construct understandings

of what should be considered personal and what should not. Adolescents may gather information about the freedom and rules that their friends have, which can be compared with the roles and boundaries that exist in their own family. (p. 79)

 Reality

Seventh grade female: The best thing about my school is the teachers and my friends. Our teachers are real neat and they like us a lot, well most of them do. I would not want to go to another school because it would be hard to get to know new people. Here I know where everything is, and I know the teachers' names and which ones are nice and which ones are mean. Sixth grade was fun because I learned a lot and got to see my friends.

McDevitt and Ormrod (2007) defined moral development as "acquiring standards about right and wrong, thinking more thoughtfully and abstractly about moral issues, and increasingly engaging in prosocial behaviors that reflect concern for other people's rights and needs" (p. 515). In their review of research related to moral development, the authors concluded that moral reasoning is characterized by general trends more than distinct stages. During ages 10–14, these trends include recognition of rules and growing awareness of individual responsibility (p. 521). McDevitt and Ormrod were careful to note that increased powers of moral reasoning do not automatically result in higher levels of moral behavior.

As the adolescents' sense of autonomy expands during this period, parenting styles that are supportive and stimulate moral reasoning have a major influence on the positive establishment of social and moral boundaries. In the quest for maturity, middle level students push against established limits. These limits may be related to areas such as what can be watched on television, what can and cannot be done to a younger brother or sister, what they can and cannot wear, where they can go, and how late they can stay out. The tendency of adolescents to

74

push limits to a moderate extent is important in establishing a true and effective identity.

It is natural for middle level students to ask teachers or parents for ideas about how to proceed on an experiment, what to say in a social situation, or what to wear—and then they promptly reject whatever is suggested. They want adult input but also want to be able to accept it or reject it on their own terms. This move from dependence to independence often causes adults to become frustrated. These same young people who press to stay out later at night with friends may still be afraid of the dark and leave a night light on when going to bed. They may be willing to work hard at difficult tasks when they can clearly see immediate benefits but be very reluctant to apply themselves to tasks for which the payoff will not come until some distant future. These vacillations from childish to adult-like behavior are natural, and if teachers and parents keep this in mind, they will be less disappointed when they experience the unevenness in young adolescent behavior.

These and other issues can become battlegrounds that are usually related more to who is in charge than to the particular issue at stake. Young adolescents often want the privileges of adults and the freedom to do what they want. Because they lack the necessary maturity to handle some of these privileges, parents rightfully draw the line and say "no." Parents and teachers not only have the right to set limits—they have a responsibility to set and enforce them. At the same time, young adolescents behave as though it is their sacred responsibility to challenge these limits. If parents and teachers do what they should do, students will do what comes naturally. They will resist, plead, confront, sulk a little, and manipulate reality ("everyone else gets to go") in order to get their way.

These confrontations are what make family allegiances appear shaky. Both parents and young adolescents may become angry, even furious, frustrated, stressed out, and a bit resentful at times. The only consolation to these interactions of varying intensity between parents and young adolescents is that relationships become more harmonious as young adolescents mature and become independent. Autonomy grows stronger as youth gain as much freedom as they can responsibly handle.

Negotiating social interactions

Students' perceptions of their levels of competence and autonomy depend greatly on the ways they think other people see them. The web of social contacts and interactions experienced by middle level students has a potent impact on the way young people think, feel, and act. As good middle level teachers know, the academic achievements of young adolescents may rise or fall due to the perceived quality of their social lives. If they feel rejected, they may invest an inordinate amount of time and energy on social matters to compensate for their sense of inadequacy, leaving less time for academic concerns. When they feel accepted by peers, young adolescents are much more likely to apply themselves to academic work.

Anthony's description of the middle level identity groups that began this chapter make it clear that this concept of "fitting in" is an important part of adolescent identity formation. Cotterell (2007) described this process as social networking and states,

> Cliques are natural groupings of peers. Members are of similar ages, have similar interests, communicate easily with one another, and spend a great deal of their time together simply enjoying one another's company. Although cliques remain valued social structures all our lives, associating in cliques is distinctively an activity that has importance in adolescence. (p. 55)

Reality

Teacher: I have certainly witnessed many of these identity changes among my seventh grade students. One thing that resonated with me was the importance of relationships to this age group. My students place a tremendous amount of importance on being accepted by their peers. Indeed, some of my students seem to value peer relationships above all else, including academics. For instance, Janice refused to come

76

to school for a week after getting kicked off the cheerleading team because she did not want to be embarrassed around her cheerleader friends. Diontravia only started staying for after-school tutoring when she saw that many of the "cool kids" were staying, too. When students do not feel that they fit in with their peers, however, this becomes their primary area of concern—they simply cannot focus on learning. Darius, an intelligent young man, has made poor grades this year because he has been so distracted by not fitting in with the other students. He has a great deal of anxiety about being picked on and is not attentive during class. Relationships with peers clearly have a great influence on a child's academic performance during the middle school years.

Acceptance by friends of the same age is a central concern in the lives of young adolescents. In the extreme, a young person may be willing to commit acts of violence, take drugs, become sexually precocious, or dependent on alcohol just to be accepted by peers. More commonly, middle level students may willingly be cruel to others, deliberately make fun of others who are different from them, or may take risks such as hassling teachers to be more accepted by their peers (Hoge, 1999). Those belonging to social groups cling to the security of that group to the point that they may yield their own individuality and behave in ways that run counter to the way they actually think and feel in order to maintain group membership.

Those who do not belong to "premier" groups form their own sub-groups. Membership in these subgroups may help members sustain themselves through what may seem to be a difficult period of life. Peer groups often take over the supportive or supplementary roles traditionally found in a family (Routledge, Mani, Pence, & Hoskins, 2001; Operario, Tschann, Flores, & Bridges, 2006). Understanding the power of peer groups may help teachers better understand why gang identity is so important to some young adolescents. A colleague once reminded us that the same dynamics that create the power of sports teams—shared goals, identifiable colors, commitment to teammates—may also describe gang membership. It is also true that a fully functioning middle school will meet all those needs.

As teachers and researchers, typically we are most concerned about those students who are the isolates. They are not isolates by choice; rather, they are rejected because they do not meet "appearance" standards or comply with conventional social norms. Acting differently, these students are perceived by their peers as "weird," "dumb," or "airheads." The result is that they are ridiculed, harassed, and humiliated. They become the ones most disconnected with school and at risk for dropping out or being involved in risk-taking behaviors (Scales, 1996; Lopez & DuBois, 2005).

Many young adolescents find it difficult to withstand peer pressure and do what they believe will please their friends, sometimes getting hurt in the process. Teachers are usually quite aware of the dramatic mood fluctuations that are related to the success or lack of it young adolescents experience in their quest for acceptance by peers.

Much has been written about the impact of media and technology on young adolescents' social interactions. One recurring theme in this area is the powerful message that encourages young people to "grow up" to be more like adults and, therefore, to do all that adults do at a younger and younger age. A major influence on this quest is the impact of the World Wide Web. A simple search by one of the authors revealed scores of Web sites dedicated to teen television, screen, and music idols. The official and unofficial Web sites provide biographies, gossip, and a multitude of video, audio, and still pictures that depict celebrities in various aspects of life. The vast majority of Web sites appear harmless and even provide useful information to adolescents. However, the darker side of the Web emerges with so many stories of adolescents left unsupervised and being influenced by Web sites dedicated to hate groups, pornography, and other unhealthy or negative influences that directly impact their behavior and identity formation.

Television, movies, teen magazines, and the Web often convey the message that children in the elementary years should dress, act, think, and feel like they are young adolescents—and that young adolescents should act like adults. This encouragement may take the form of gender stereotyping that reinforces behaviors of aggression and autonomy for boys and nurtures emotional and passive behavior for girls. At a minimum, media and technology have created a very wide range of opportunities for social interactions at younger ages, all of which may impact young adolescents' search for an identity.

Facebook, originally started in 2004 as a college community networking tool, has grown into the most popular communication tool on the Internet and illustrates the extension of social network theory into the digital age. In 2006 Facebook opened up its doors to all potential Internet users. Initially an individual joins a Facebook network, then after setting up a profile, begins to "friend" individuals within and beyond their network. Individuals who wish to extend their network of "friends" then search the network for individuals or groups and submit a friend request directly to a person within the network. The request can be accepted, denied, or simply not acted on. Accepting, denying, or "defriending" a particular person has a powerful impact. This form of social networking allows interaction via a multimedia platform that includes providing personal information about such matters as a person's religious and political viewpoints, activities, interests, music, favorite television shows, and books read. Additionally, participants can build "walls" where friends can post a variety of information. Facebook additionally allows online chats.

As popularity of Facebook, Twitter, and related digital experiences increases, the old dilemmas of privacy, independence, and parental oversight have gained greater urgency. More and more parents are setting up their own profiles and are connecting to their own children or their children's friends' profiles. If communicated appropriately, parents can filter and provide guidance related to a variety of issues that arise daily. However, the sudden emergence of parents into this digital network presents adolescents with the age-old complaint that "my parents don't understand me."

Over the past decade, a second form of social communication that has become available for young adolescents is the cell phone. Once a luxury item, the cell phone has quickly turned into a "necessity"

At break time, students will activate some of the many technological devices they possess.

for youth, seemingly regardless of their personal financial status. The authors' discussions with middle level parents reveal that some students text thousands of times per month. A new written language of abbreviations has been created informally and varies among social groups. One group of middle school friends were observed physically sitting within a foot or two of each other at an event. Each student was frantically texting a friend not present about the latest "drama of the moment." Texting policies and "netiquette" are quickly becoming fixtures in middle school student code and conduct manuals. The speed and availability of digital communications have increased the pace and complexity of young adolescents' personal, social, and moral development and amplified the need for security, success, and support.

Providing security, success, and support

Those three words—security, success, and support—encapsulate the personal needs of middle level students. While young adolescents often seem self-assured, interviews and survey responses indicate that most of them need to feel secure. Among the top fears they often list are the loss of a parent, acts of violence, and disease. As children, they may have known these fears; but as adolescents, they may dwell on them. Even when they manage to put such fears in perspective, their thoughts reveal a mixture of optimism and anxiety. The following "bio-poem" written by a seventh grader is an illustration.

80

Janet
Cheerful, friendly, outgoing, musical,
Daughter of Mr. & Mrs. _____,
Likes the Jonas Brothers, summer, playing sports,
Feels good around people, happy most of the time,
Sad when it rains,
Fears going new places, meeting new people, death,
Would like to see the world in peace,
Smiling faces all the time,
The Jonas Brothers in person.
Resident of Winston-Salem.

Janet's thoughts reveal a combination of child-like joy and adult-like fears. The need for security has grown even more pronounced with the cultural and societal changes of recent decades. There was a time when many young adolescents felt the presence of a "safety net" of family and friends. Even though they experienced the uncertainties of passage into adulthood, they were aware of the security provided by parents, siblings, grandparents, other relatives, and probably a familiar community where many people knew and cared for them. This sense of relational security extends into an individual's perception of happiness. Magen's (1998) cross-cultural study on adolescents' perception of happiness found that adolescents experience joy within relationships with peers and family members. These experiences were centered on feelings of being trusted. Although many young adolescents may feel this "safety net" as one factor in the experience of happiness, all too many others feel the anxieties of disrupted homes and economic distress. They may have moved, attended several schools, lived in different neighborhoods, or never really known grandparents or an extended family. These factors may accentuate the loneliness of adolescence and the need for providing as secure a school environment as possible.

A related need is support. As they begin to define their identity and break away from parents, most young adolescents need to establish close relationships with other adults. Teachers often fill this role.

Eighth grade male: Everybody thinks Coach K is the greatest teacher and coach. He can explain games in a way that you really know how to play them, and he chooses games that are really fun to play. Sometimes, like in badminton, he'd take on the whole class. He'd be on one side and we'd all be on the other. He had this way of talking that made you know you were all right. He also had a way of picking on the goofiest guy in the class. We'd say if Coach K picked on you that meant he liked you. Sometimes, I wish that Coach K would pick on me.

Young adolescents often seek opportunities to talk to a favorite teacher.

Teachers often observe this need for support when students begin to "hang around" their classrooms before or after school for little apparent reason. Sometimes, they just want to talk about their interests and adventures, tell bad jokes, or just sit and listen to others—anything. Some young adolescents become very close to their scout leaders, coaches, or Sunday school teachers. They want to find adults who will accept them and have "adult" conversations. They often find it easier to talk with a teacher than with their parents, especially about the changes in their lives and the ways they feel about them. This need for support is more than acceptance; it is a need to feel a part of the world of adults.

Interviewer: Think about the teacher you like the least and describe that teacher for me.

Fourteen-year-old female: She was pretty mean. Anytime we had something to do, she'd just tell you to do it, no questions asked or answered. She wouldn't even let you go see the guidance counselor if you had a problem. She went over some of the work, but most of it you had to get on your own.

Interviewer: Would this teacher listen to your problems, or did you ever feel like going to her with your problems?

Student: No, I saw what happened to the other kids. They went to the office for just asking one little question.

In addition to security and support, young adolescents need to experience success. They need to feel that they are valuable, able, and responsible. Positive academic and social experiences nurture self-concept. When they feel accepted by their teachers and peers, they simply are more likely to do well in school. Common sense as well as research support this reality.

Even more powerful in determining achievement is how they feel about themselves as learners. It has long been noted that one of the best predictors of academic achievement is self-concept. Children who finish first grade convinced that they can read well and are successful are far, far more likely to be good readers in the sixth grade than those who feel that they are poor readers. We believe that the same concept is true with other areas or subjects.

Conclusion

Answers to the questions "Who am I?" and "Where do I fit in?" vary greatly among young adolescents. Students form a healthy sense of identity when they learn to see themselves as more competent, have a greater sense of autonomy, and interact positively with peers and adults. As we have suggested in earlier chapters, the most successful schools and the most successful teachers in the middle grades are those who meet their students' needs for security, support, and success in a proactive manner.

Despite their apparent buoyancy, young adolescents are fragile, perhaps more fragile than at other times in their lives. The changes they experience in personal, social, and moral development can help them grow stronger—or put them at greater risk. The same is true of the ways they experience transitions in physical and sexual development, issues we addressed in an earlier chapter. Successful teachers address these developmental needs in the daily life of their classrooms. Over the years, we have learned a great deal about the ways exemplary teachers orchestrate these dynamics by creating connections with their students, insights we will highlight in our next chapter.

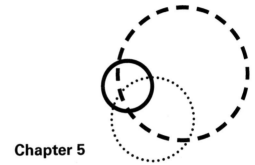

Chapter 5

Promoting Harmony in Middle Level Classrooms

The complexity of the developmental changes that young adolescents experience underscores our commitment to provide programs and practices that are specifically designed for young adolescents themselves. Because these changes are so dynamic, middle level classrooms must be responsive and supportive. As we have noted throughout the book, it is this responsiveness that creates harmony. Becoming a responsive teacher begins with gaining a full understanding of young adolescents and an appreciation for their individuality.

Shared expectations for good teaching

Teachers who seek to meet the needs of their students more effectively would do well by reviewing anew the characteristics of young adolescents as they play out in today's society. Chapters 2–4 sought to do this. Then teachers should consider the characteristics of good teaching that have emerged from research. For more than 30 years, National Middle School Association (NMSA) has served as a clearinghouse and policy source for research on teaching at the middle level. Over time, the organization has distilled the most important insights from research into the *Teacher Preparation Standards* (NMSA, 2005). These standards guide middle level teacher preparation programs and offer specific definitions of the knowledge, dispositions, and performances that characterize good teaching at the middle level. Figure 5.1 offers a summary of these expectations.

The seven standards summarize what middle level teachers know and do to be successful. The first standard, Young Adolescent Development, provides the foundation for the six that follow. To consider philosophy, develop curriculum, identify content, plan instruction, connect with family and community, and grow as professionals, teachers need to have a full understanding of students as a foundation. The essence of good teaching is being responsive to their needs.

As teachers and researchers, we have studied these dynamics in classrooms enough to know that our most inspiring teachers had a theory of action; that is, they made decisions based on their personal values, philosophy, and professional wisdom (Strahan, Smith, McElrath, & Toole, 2001; Strahan, & Layell, 2006; Strahan, Faircloth, Cope, & Hundley 2007). Teachers in the case studies conducted by these researchers shared similar values yet enacted them in different ways to respond to the needs of their students (Strahan, 2008).

In the pages following Figure 5.1, we present a framework that synthesizes these insights with the results of research that has been cited throughout this text. Using this framework, we describe middle level practices that promote harmony and provide some examples as "featured performances." Just as an orchestra sometimes spotlights a particular instrument or performer, these featured performances represent exemplary practices that characterize harmony in action.

Figure 5.1
Expectations for Good Teaching

NMSA Standard	Expectations—Middle level teachers understand . . .
1. Young Adolescent Development	the major concepts, principles, theories, and research related to young adolescent development, and they provide opportunities that support student development and learning.
2. Middle Level Philosophy and School Organization	the major concepts, principles, theories, and research underlying the philosophical foundations of developmentally responsive middle level programs and schools, and they work successfully within these organizational components.
3. Middle Level Curriculum and Assessment	the major concepts, principles, theories, standards, and research related to middle level curriculum and assessment, and they use this knowledge in their practice.
4. Middle Level Teaching Fields	and use the central concepts, tools of inquiry, standards, and structures of content in their chosen teaching fields, and they create meaningful learning experiences that develop all young adolescents' competence in subject matter and skills.
5. Middle Level Instruction and Assessment	and use the major concepts, principles, theories, and research related to effective instruction and assessment, and they employ a variety of strategies for a developmentally appropriate climate to meet the varying abilities and learning styles of all young adolescents.
6. Family and Community Involvement	the major concepts, principles, theories, and research related to working collaboratively with family and community members, and they use that knowledge to maximize the learning of all young adolescents.
7. Middle Level Professional Roles	the complexity of teaching young adolescents, and they engage in practices and behaviors that develop their competence as professionals.

Classroom communities that nurture connections

Just as musical harmony results from the blending of sounds, harmony in the classroom occurs when teachers create innumerable connections with young people—kind words, supportive expressions, simple courtesies, and carefully crafted, engaging lesson activities. When these connections grow strong enough, students perceive a "critical mass" of sorts, and then, even the most reluctant students will engage in learning activities. Responsive teaching is the synergy of these relationships. While the ways successful teachers connect with students vary, all reflect the core values that guide their decisions. Figure 5.2 presents a graphic representation of these essential dynamics.

From the bottom up, this figure illustrates the practices that enhance the "personal and academic momentum" introduced in Chapter 1. The process begins when teachers create learning communities that invite students and build trust. They engage students in informal conversations, learn more about them as individuals, and come to understand their academic strengths. By actively listening, they learn students' thoughts and ideas. As students come to trust their teachers and classmates, they cross a threshold and begin to engage more frequently in lesson activities, especially those that scaffold instruction and teach strategies explicitly. Because they trust their teachers and their classmates, students will assess their own work more candidly and willingly seek guidance from their teachers. They also interact more positively with other people. From these positive experiences, they move to setting goals, making plans, and assessing their progress more specifically. As they gain confidence, students will experiment with new learning behaviors, thoughts, and feelings until they reach that significant point where they have enough self-efficacy and self-regulation to learn more independently.

The climate and context that are necessary for these steps to take place is characterized by four conditions identified in Figure 5.2. At each step of the way, these four conditions or sources of energy fuel these dynamics. As emphasized previously, **physical and emotional safety** are essential prerequisites for learning, and good teachers do everything they can

Figure 5.2

The Dynamics of Developing Personal and Academic Connections with Young Adolescents

1. Physical and emotional safety,

2. personal support,

3. responsive instruction, and

4. dialogue that connect with students' needs.

Growing stronger academically—As students gain confidence in themselves, they assess their progress more candidly, monitor their engagement, refine their goals, and improve their skills, thereby increasing personal and academic momentum and improving achievement.

Experimenting with new behaviors, thoughts, and feelings—As they address goals and enact plans, students find it helpful to have choices of assignments. They can consider alternatives, tap prior knowledge, try strategies in different ways, and connect them with real-world experiences.

Setting goals and planning—As students engage more frequently with learning strategies, teachers encourage them to set personal and academic goals, make plans, and assume more responsibility for their learning.

Engaging in learning activities—Once trusting relationships develop, students can begin to take some risks and engage in specific learning activities, especially those that "scaffold" strategy instruction and provide models of strategies in action. As they take these small steps, they begin to expect teachers to provide honest assessments of their work and give them explicit guidance, supportive responses that help them strengthen their sense of identity as learners.

••••••••**Threshold for Creating Connections**••••••••••••

Creating classroom communities that nurture trusting relationships— Caring relationships are the key to engaging young adolescents in lessons. Successful teachers cultivate trust by involving students in conversations that allow them to learn more about students as individuals, to understand their academic strengths and needs, and to encourage shared responsibility. They also promote positive relationships among students so that they support each other and learn to work in teams.

to make sure that their students are physically safe and protected from psychological harm. Throughout the text, we have shown that ongoing **personal support** reminds students that their teachers and classmates care about them as individuals—who they are and how they feel. **Responsive instruction** helps them increase their cognitive understandings and strengthen their skills of self-regulation. Our analysis of reasoning development in Chapter 2 suggests that students are most engaged with lesson activities tailored to their learning strengths and structured to build concepts. **Dialogue** regarding personal and academic choices helps them internalize a sense of responsibility for their learning. As this growth spiral strengthens, teachers increase the levels of challenge, foster an even greater sense of "connectedness" among students, and strengthen momentum.

To illustrate further these dynamics, in the next section we offer examples from case studies (Strahan, 2008) and follow that with other examples of ways to provide these key conditions: physical and emotional safety, personal support, responsive instruction, and ways to structure dialogue on personal and academic choices.

Harmony in action

Last year, I couldn't keep track of my work. I lost homework on the way to school or left it at home. I got in a lot of trouble. This year I'm staying out of trouble. I have more friends, some of them are better, some still get in trouble, but not as much as they used to. I'm on the ABC honor roll, so I get to go on the honor roll trips. That's something I've never done before.

(Randy, 01/05)

As an eighth grader, Randy's academic engagement increased dramatically. He rarely got in trouble. He became a leader on community service projects. He even qualified for the honor roll, and his scores on statewide tests rose significantly. Randy, with the support of his teachers, reversed the negative dynamics that had plagued him in the past. This story demonstrated a pattern of performance that has grown clearer in recent research reports. A detailed case study chronicled these accomplishments (Strahan, Faircloth, Cope, &

Hundley 2007). A brief summary of this case will illustrate how two caring teachers helped Randy develop stronger personal and academic momentum. (See Figure 5.2, p. 89.)

To encourage self-confidence and involvement, teachers Nancy and Terri began the school year with activities designed to create a sense of community. On the first day of school, they established a daily routine that featured classroom meetings. In these meetings, they defined their expectations for team behavior and procedures explicitly, and reviewed and demonstrated rules. They planned outdoor learning experiences that built camaraderie with hacky-sack competitions and team football games. They created lessons that required teamwork and peer tutoring, held conversations about teams and working together, and guided reflections about team events. During class meetings, they planned team field trips with students making the basic decisions about these trips.

To make teamwork more concrete and specific, they asked students to plan community service activities. Students decided to volunteer at a nearby elementary school, an elder care facility, or a local soup kitchen. Other students chose to work on the school grounds. Randy quickly became the leader of the team that worked on the school garden with students from the special education class. "We show them how we can garden and improve the community. It's a benefit for them to get out and do stuff that they normally can't do. I enjoy doing that, helping people and doing something outside" (01/05).

If students misbehaved, Nancy and Terri conducted extensive individual conversations with them. Early in the year, Randy became distracted during a math lesson and had to miss his service learning time. He reported to us later that this was a turning point for him. He decided he did not want to miss his service learning time again and said, "If I do my part in the garden, I get a reward and can come back next time. You show teachers you're responsible, they let you come back. You have to be trusted by them so you can leave class. Rewards work better than ISS and OSS" (01/05). For Randy, this realization became a threshold event. He did not miss service learning again for the rest of the year.

Nancy and Terri developed project assignments that addressed inquiry-oriented, student-selected issues. When reading *The Outsiders,* for example, they asked students to identify ways that the social dynamics of high school in the 1960s were similar to those they experienced in middle school. The teachers raised questions related to conflict resolution, analyzed choices characters made, and examined the consequences of those decisions. In several interviews, Randy described how he was engaging in learning activities in ways that were new for him. Project assignments encouraged Randy to take risks, learn new ways of thinking, and make personal connections. His successes with these activities strengthened his self-efficacy. Even when he perceived that tasks were difficult, he wanted to do well and could be candid about his performance.

Nancy and Terri developed a daily routine that featured goal-setting and reflective writing assignments. Each morning, students helped decide on the daily agenda. These morning meetings often centered on the attitudes and behaviors that would lead to success with the day's events. Each grading period, teachers asked students to identify, in writing, their own goals for the progress report period and then to reflect on how well they believed they had accomplished those goals. At the end of the day, they often asked students to reflect on a decision scenario that might put these values into action. Opportunities to set goals and reflect on decision scenarios helped Randy think through the choices he was making and assume more responsibility for his learning.

As Randy reflected on his work, he became aware that he was using specific learning strategies. This heightened sense of self-regulation reinforced his growing confidence, encouraged him to think at deeper levels, and led him to set higher goals for himself. Randy's new habits of mind served him well. He completed eighth grade with good grades and qualified for the honor roll for the first time. He made dramatic gains on his end-of-year achievement tests, gaining 16 points in mathematics and eight points in reading, far surpassing the expectation of four developmental scale points per year. When we interviewed him after his first semester of ninth grade, he told us

There is a real big difference at the high school because of changing classes and finding all the buildings. Everything keeps getting harder, but I'm doing pretty good. I'm passing all my classes now (two weeks into the second semester). I'm in a drama class for art credit. We have to interact with people, and that helps me improve my speaking skills and not be scared. I used not to interact with many people. (02/06)

Our study with these two teachers and Randy and his classmates documented many of the ways that teachers and students can work together to strengthen personal and academic momentum (Strahan, Faircloth, Cope, & Hundley, 2007). As seventh graders, Randy and his friends displayed a survival orientation toward school—acting busy, forgetting homework, and disrupting class as ways to avoid work. Nancy and Terri worked hard to understand the students as individuals and identify their academic strengths and needs. They planned lessons that drew on these strengths and scaffolded strategy instruction to build higher levels of understanding. At they same time, they encouraged shared responsibility and held students accountable for their actions. They promoted higher levels of trust by providing ongoing personal support, giving candid feedback, and promoting dialogue regarding academic and personal choices. As the year progressed and the learning community grew stronger, Nancy and Terri provided increasingly challenging tasks, fostering stronger academic momentum.

In this environment, Randy and many of his classmates developed higher levels of both skill and will. They assumed more responsibility for their own learning and understood how to invest energy in lesson activities. As they began to understand concepts in deeper ways, new insights kindled higher levels of self-efficacy and self-regulation. Stronger skills and tangible moments of success convinced them they could make progress. This sense of momentum fueled stronger levels of engagement. As a result, Randy and many of his classmates entered high school with greater confidence and persistence.

Practices that promote harmony

In this illustration, Nancy and Terri created the four essential dynamics that enabled their students to develop stronger personal and academic momentum: 1) physical and emotional safety, 2) personal support, 3) responsive instruction, and 4) dialogue regarding personal and academic choices. Their practices addressed the needs of their particular students and may not automatically transfer to other classrooms, but there are many ways that middle level teachers can produce these essential dynamics. We conclude our text with examples of practices that provide physical and emotional safety, offer personal support, deliver responsive instruction, and foster dialogue regarding both personal and academic choices.

Providing physical and emotional safety

All learners need a safe classroom environment. With young adolescents negotiating numerous physical and sexual developmental changes, this need becomes especially important. The classroom should be a safe haven in a world that may sometimes seem lonely and frightening. Teachers who understand students' needs, interests, and concerns can help them examine issues related to health and wellness, debunk myths, and provide factual information. During the transition from childhood to adulthood, students naturally ask themselves many questions about their values and beliefs. They try to sort through the messages they receive about what it means to be good, to care for others, and to take care of themselves. Teachers play an essential role in this process and can create classroom climates that promote respect and responsibility.

Featured performance: AA across the day: Advisor-advisee programs are designed to provide opportunities for self-exploration. Students are not forced to "share" everything. Some reflective activities are theirs alone. Discussions provide a chance to hear how others think and feel without taking excessive risks. In successful advisory programs, students learn as much about themselves as they do about each other. In his review of research on advisor-advisee programs, Anfara (2006) described a wide variety of approaches and concluded, "structural differences are not what is truly important. What matters are the communication,

94

community, and caring relationships that develop as a result of effective advisory programs" (p. 55).

Teachers can integrate these central processes in all subjects and in various events throughout the school day (Van Hoose, 1991). For example, in language arts, the teacher might ask students to create a "Me Bag," decorated on the outside with drawings that portray scenes from their lives and carrying small objects that symbolize some of their most important values. Sharing these in a show and tell fashion allows students to learn more about each other. The teacher can then extend this activity to provide prompts for writing or examples for character bags that portray scenes and values from novels. In science, teachers can naturally infuse discussions about body awareness into lessons on human

Discussions of students' personal-social concerns and interests occur in the regular meetings of advisory groups.

growth and development. In mathematics, lessons on statistics can focus on questions of interest selected by the class, a survey of issues faced in transition to high school, or graphs of favorite video games. In social studies, class meetings can provide a natural forum for considering issues of governance, beginning with issues selected by the teacher and evolving to real-time issues suggested by students—how to deal with bullies, for example. Lessons like these provide natural moments for students to discuss topics that matter to them and learn more about each other. Teams that practice thematic units or curriculum integration can more readily develop these four central processes or dynamics.

Offering ongoing personal support

Early adolescence is a very fragile time for many students. Many feel a heightened sense of anxiety about their academic, social, and athletic abilities; on one hand, they want attention and recognition; on the other, they want to be part of a crowd. The types of attention and confirmation they receive in the school environment are especially important. Physical, social, intellectual, and personal changes create a kaleidoscopic situation in which they try to determine who they are and how they relate to the "adult world." One of the most meaningful ways that teachers can help students learn more about themselves and others is in service learning.

Featured performance: Service learning. The concept of service learning has long been a part of middle level education but has received increased attention in the first decade of the 21st century. Across the years, teachers, administrators, and parents have worked with young adolescents in incorporating various ways that students can contribute to their schools and communities, providing the "real" experiences young adolescents seek. Scales (1999) believed that formal programs featuring service learning can address this need "in a powerful fashion." His study of the impact of service learning on more than 1000 middle school students in three different programs showed that these experiences have positive benefits for students when such experiences meet three key conditions:

1) Students spend a significant amount of time engaged in service learning (more than 31 hours per year).
2) Students have opportunities to reflect on their experiences.
3) Students feel such experiences are linked with their classes.

(p. 40)

Students who reported experiences that met these conditions
- Significantly improved in their sense of duty to others.
- Significantly increased their sense that they could make a difference when helping others.
- Maintained their sense that school provided developmental opportunities such as decision making and recognition.
- Declined less than other students in their commitment to class work.
- Improved somewhat in pursuing good grades. (pp. 40–41)

Scales' results confirm our observations that students form positive values when caring adults provide them systematic opportunities to care for their classmates, other adults, and their communities (Strahan, Faircloth, Cope, & Hundley, 2007).

Smith (2005) described an excellent example of the benefits of service learning. Teachers at Pine Point Middle School in Stoning, Connecticut, crafted an experiential learning project that called for eighth graders to make at least seven visits to a participating community organization. Students kept a journal chronicling their experiences and read a book that related to issues addressed by the agency they selected. Teachers conducted a series of advisory support group discussions to help students reflect on their experiences. Community service experiences flowed naturally into a comprehensive writing assignment followed by an oral presentation to a panel of classmates and faculty judges. Students generated a wealth of work products that "expressed new confidence in their ability to tackle complex tasks, communicate their ideas clearly to others, and think on their feet" (p. 25).

Lessons that deliver responsive instruction

As we noted in Chapter 2, early adolescence is a critical time in the development of the mind. The intertwined connections that characterize thinking provide a challenge for teachers who hope to nurture understanding, especially when the concepts emphasized in the curriculum may seem distant and abstract to students. Fortunately, researchers have identified a set of teaching practices that have proven successful in guiding students in creating new connections.

In a synthesis of research on learning, Bransford, Brown, and Cocking (2000) concluded,

> Children are both problem solvers and problem generators: children attempt to solve problems presented to them and they also seek novel challenges. They refine and improve their problem-solving strategies not only in the face of failure, but also by building on prior successes. They persist because success and understanding are motivating in their own right. Adults help make connections between new situations and familiar ones for children.

Children's curiosity and persistence are supported by adults who
- Direct their attention.
- Structure their experiences.
- Support their learning attempts.
- Regulate the complexity and difficulty levels of information for them. (p. 112)

These four descriptors provide an excellent definition of "scaffolding," a term that has become a powerful metaphor for good teaching.

Featured performance: Scaffolded instruction. Just as a construction crew builds a scaffold to frame a new structure, teachers design instructional scaffolds to frame the development of ideas and concepts. As Tomlinson (2003) has suggested, scaffolding is an instructional support system that guides intellectual growth.

We scaffold growth when we follow a particular logic of thought. First, we know precisely where students need to arrive at the end of a lesson, a unit or a year . . . Then, we determine where each student is at the moment in relation to the goals and in her personal development. Finally, we take action to ensure that each student grows as vigorously as possible . . . .
In other words, we ensure catalysts for growth—we scaffold it.
(p. 65)

Successful teachers create scaffolds to guide students in "building" concepts. They often begin with opportunities for students to think and talk about what they already know about the topic and then provide activities that build motivation and readiness for new concepts. For example, one teacher we observed began a lesson on "balancing equations" with a discussion of the idea of balance. When one student suggested that "you have to balance on a balance beam," the teacher asked him to come to the front of the class and demonstrate walking on a thin line. She then asked students to describe what they saw. Several students suggested that when he leaned one way, he had to put his arm out the other way. They defined "balance" as "evening things out." She then used a balance scale and weights to demonstrate a different type of balance. Students then defined "balance" as keeping both sides even. At this point, the teacher demonstrated how to balance several equations. Students then generated a mathematical definition. In this lesson, they did not start reading and answering questions and problems in the text until they had generated the critical concept they needed for successfully doing so.

These types of scaffolded lessons promote higher levels of student engagement. Among the many findings to emerge from the Far West Lab studies in the 1970s was the distinction between time-on-task (often busywork) and "Academic Learning Time (ALT)." Researchers discovered that the best measure of student learning was the time spent engaged in tasks that students viewed as meaningful and that they felt they could complete successfully. During reading time, for example, those students who have books that they want to read and have time to read will improve their proficiency in reading. If a student reads actively for 20 minutes during a half-hour block of time, he accumulates 20 minutes of ALT. If a student spends 25 minutes looking for a book or just "turning pages" and only five minutes really reading, he accumulates only five minutes of ALT. Over the course of a school year, the amount of ALT that a teacher encourages is directly related to how much students learn. Since researchers first framed the construct of ALT, studies have continued to demonstrate the power of time engaged with high quality tasks (Masci, 2008).

We observed an excellent example of ALT and engagement in a lesson called "Pizza Hut Math." While studying decimals, the class was divided into groups, and the teacher gave students actual menus from Pizza Hut. Each group selected a waiter or waitress to record each order. Students added to figure the bill, multiplied to determine sales tax, and divided to determine each person's share. They "practiced" the social skills of ordering from a menu and working together. Thus, all students practiced their math skills in an innovative fashion.

Fostering meaningful dialogue

One powerful insight that underlies all aspects of development is the importance of conversation in making sense of experience. While most of us like to think aloud, thinking aloud is especially powerful during early adolescence. There is validity in the saying, "How do I know what I think until I hear what I say?" Not only do students need to discuss the changes they are experiencing, but the dialogue itself is a central vehicle for comprehension. Dialogue is purposeful conversation, talk focused on understanding. Learning to think through decisions and connect choices with consequences requires dialogue.

Featured performance: Systematic decision scenarios. Successful middle level teachers have developed a number of problem-solving frameworks to encourage logical decision making. For example, most science teachers emphasize a step-by-step "scientific method" for investigating science problems in their classrooms. Mathematics teachers routinely employ varied heuristics for problem solving. Using decision scenarios, teachers can enrich these frameworks to help students solve academic problems and approach real world situations more thoughtfully.

Edelson, Tarnoff, Schwille, Brouzas, and Switzer (2006) developed an approach to teaching environmental science that provides an explicit strategy for making decisions to create contexts for learning science concepts. Their Stakeholder Consequences Decision-Making (SCDM) process features four stages of analysis. In the first stage, teachers guide students in establishing basic criteria for deciding on the outcomes. Next, students identify possible consequences and apply their understanding of scientific concepts to create a "cascading consequences chart," which displays "chains of causes and effects" (p. 41). In the third stage, students assess the impact of their decision options on stakeholders. In the final stage, students weigh the impacts on stakeholders based on their values. Charting choices and consequences at each stage allows students to see how different values lead to different decisions and different outcomes.

Edelson et al. (2006) illustrated this process by describing a decision scenario in which an environmental science class considered how best to build a new school in an area of Florida that is a habitat for gopher tortoises. Students began by charting space requirements for the school and habitat requirements for the tortoises. Next they designed different permutations for school facilities, created scale drawings, and developed three site plans. For each option they constructed charts to show the consequences of each scenario. After assessing the impact for stakeholders and identifying their values, they evaluated the three options and justified their final decision in presentations using the artifacts they created. The authors concluded,

> The SCDM process offers students the opportunity to apply their content understanding in context and provides teachers with a window into their students' thinking. Equally important, it can help prepare students to make the complex decisions that they will be called to make throughout their lives. (p. 44)

Once students have learned a systematic approach to making decisions like SCDM, teachers can extend the process to analyze decisions students make in a wide range of personal situations as well as in academic contexts. Students can use this framework to analyze decisions made by characters in stories, by historical figures, by scientists, or by mathematicians. As they become more familiar with the process, they can analyze real-world situations in which they must think through the choices they make and process these choices in writing, discussions, or debates. For example, a group of eighth graders developed the flow chart on page 102 to describe how they viewed their options in deciding whether or not to invest time and energy in preparing for a high stakes test required by their school district.

In lessons like these, students have opportunities to hear teachers and classmates think aloud. They can form stronger notions of how adults make good decisions and compare the process of thoughtful deliberation to impulsive actions. When conducted in a safe environment, with strong personal support and clear instructional guidance, dialogue sessions can help young adolescents understand themselves better and develop skills for addressing personal and academic problems more successfully.

A Sample Flow Chart for Mapping "Choices and Consequences"

Situation: Test Prep—To Try or Not to Try

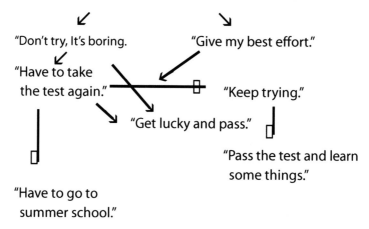

A final word

Throughout this text, we have analyzed the developmental characteristics of young adolescents and the opportunities for responsive teaching these characteristics offer for educators. We have documented ways that successful teachers create connections with students and make their classrooms places where students are physically and emotionally safe, where teachers and classmates provide ongoing personal support, where instruction is responsive to students' needs, and where students have opportunities to engage in dialogue regarding personal and academic choices. As these dynamics come to characterize the classroom culture, an even greater sense of "connectedness" among students and teachers evolves. Students gain the desired personal and academic momentum accordingly.

These dynamics of responsiveness create many, many moments of harmony. Mahatma Gandhi once wrote that "Happiness is when what you think, what you say, and what you do are in harmony." As we bring this book to a close, it strikes us that his description of harmony is very similar to the definition of flow discussed in Chapter 1: "Flow is what people feel when they enjoy what they are doing, when they would not want to do anything else" (Csikszentmihalyi & Nakamura, 1989, p. 55). Students and teachers alike appreciate "aha moments" and the connections that characterize moments of flow in classrooms. We should remember that all descriptions of flow and harmony emphasize living in the present tense. Many times in education, we encourage students to study something for future use. While there may be good reasons to think of education as an investment, we believe that the most important moments in classrooms have their value in the here and now as teachers and students make connections with ideas and each other.

In our work with middle level schools, we have been inspired by the legions of dedicated professionals whose classrooms are harmonious learning environments in which young adolescents acquire a full and meaningful education. We hope the materials in this book will inspire new and experienced teachers to follow their lead and establish procedures and practices that will promote harmony—and achievement—in middle level classrooms.

Bibliography

Aalsma, M. C., Lapsley, D. K., & Flannery, D. J. (2006). Personal fables, narcissism, and adolescent adjustment. *Psychology in the Schools, 43*(4), 481–491.

Alvermann, D. E. (2009). Sociocultural constructions of adolescence and young people's literacies. In L. Christenbury, R. Bomer, & P. Smagorinsky (Eds.) *Handbook of adolescent literacy research* (pp. 14–28). New York: The Guilford Press.

Andrews, P. G., Caskey, M. M., & Anfara, V. A., Jr. (2007). *Research summary: Characteristics of exemplary schools for young adolescents.* Retrieved January 31, 2008, from http://www.nmsa.org/Research/ResearchSummaries/ ExemplarySchools/tabid/256/Default.aspx

Anfara, V. A., Jr. (2006). Advisor-advisee programs: Important but problematic. *Middle School Journal, 40*(2), 54–60.

Arth, A. (1992, November 8). Presentation at National Middle School Association Conference, San Antonio, TX.

Ata, R., Ludden, A., & Lally, M. (2007). The effects of gender and family, friend, and media influences on eating behaviors and body image during adolescence [Electronic version]. *Journal of Youth & Adolescence, 36*(8), 1024–1037.

Backes, J., Ralston, A., & Ingwalson, G. (1999). Middle level reform: The impact on student achievement. *Research in Middle Level Education Quarterly, 22*(3) 43–57.

Balk, D. E. (1995). *Adolescent development: Early through late adolescence.* Pacific Grove, CA: Brooks Grove Publishing.

Barnes, G., Hoffman, J., Welte, J., Farrell, M., & Dintcheff, B. (2007). Adolescents' time use: Effects on substance use, delinquency, and sexual behavior. *Journal of Youth & Adolescence, 36*(5), 697–710.

Blum, R. W. (2005, April). A case for school connectedness. *Educational Leadership.* 16–20.

Bransford, J., Brown, A., & Cocking, R. (2000). *How people learn.* Washington, DC: National Academy Press.

Brown, D. F., & Canniff, M. (2007). Designing curricular experiences that promote young adolescents' cognitive growth. *Middle School Journal, 39*(1), 16–23.

Brown, D. F., & Leamen, H. L. (2007). Recognizing and responding to young adolescents' ethnic identity development. In S. Mertens, V. Afara, Jr., & M. Caskey (Eds.), *The young adolescent and the middle school* (pp. 219–236). Charlotte, NC: Information Age Publishing.

Bruce, D. L. (2009). Reading and writing video: Media literacy and adolescents. In L. Christenbury, R. Bomer, and P. Smagorinsky (Eds.), *Handbook of adolescent literacy research* (pp. 287–306). New York: The Guilford Press.

Canfield, J., & Wells, H. C. (1976). *100 Ways to enhance self-concept in the classroom.* Englewood Cliffs, NJ: Prentice-Hall.

Caskey, M. M., & Anfara, V.A., Jr. (2007). *Research summary: Young adolescents' developmental characteristics.* Retrieved April 27, 2008, from http://www.nmsa. org/Research/ResearchSummaries/DevelopmentalCharacteristics/tabid/1414/ Default.aspx

Caskey, M. M., & Ruben, B. (2007). Under construction: The young adolescent brain. In S. Mertens, V.A. Anfara, Jr., & M. M. Caskey (Eds.), *The young adolescent and the middle school* (pp. 47–72). Charlotte, NC: Information Age Publishing.

Children's Hospital Boston (2007). *Growth milestones for teens. Children's Hospital Boston in association with the Harvard Medical School.* Retrieved January 31, 2008, from http://www.childrenshospital.org/az/Site1720/mainpageS1720P0.html

Cichucki, P. H. (2007). Inquiring adolescent minds want to know: "What is happening to me?" *Montessori Life, 19*(4), 20–22.

Cotterell, J. (2007). *Social networks in youth and adolescence.* New York: Routledge.

Cromer, B., & Harel, Z. (2000). Adolescents: At risk for osteoporosis? [Electronic version]. *Clinical Pediatrics, 39*(10), 565–575.

Cross, P. K. (1999). *Learning is about making connections.* The Cross Papers Number 3. Laguna Hills, CA: League for Innovation in the Community College, and Princeton, NJ: Educational Testing Service.

Cross, W. E., Jr. (1991). *Shades of black: Diversity in African-American identity.* Philadelphia, Temple University Press.

Csikszentmihalyi, M. (1990). Literacy and intrinsic motivation. *Daedalus, 119* (2), 115–140.

Csikszentmihalyi, M., & Nakamura, J. (1989). The dynamics of intrinsic motivation: A study of adolescents. *Research on Motivation in Education, 3,* 45–71.

Cushman, K. (2003) *Fires in the bathroom: Advice for teachers from high school students.* New York: New Press.

Daddis, C. (2008). Influence of close friends on the boundaries of adolescent personal authority. *Journal of Research on Adolescence, 18,* 75–98.

Dusek, J., & McIntyre, J. (2003). Self-concept and self-esteem development. In G. Adams, & M. Berzonsky (Eds), *Blackwell handbook of adolescence.* Malden, MA: Blackwell Publishing Company.

Edelson, D. C., Tarnoff, A., Schwille, K., Brouzas, M., & Switzer, A. (2006). Learning to make systematic decisions. *The Science Teacher, 73*(4), 40–45.

Elkind, D. (1967). Egocentrism in adolescence. *Child Development, 38,* 1025–1034.

Erb, T. (Ed.). (2005). *This We Believe in action: Implementing successful middle level schools.* Westerville, OH: National Middle School Association.

Erickson, E. H. (1968). *Identity: Youth and crisis.* New York: Norton.

Farrington, V. T., L'Esperance, M., & Mazingo, S. (2006). Rural school improvement networks. In G. Ponder & D. Strahan (Eds.), *Deep change: Reforming schools for significance and test success* (pp. 229–254). Austin, TX: Information Age Publishing, Inc.

Felner, R. D., Jackson, A. W., Kasak, D., Mulhall, P., Brand, S., & Flowers, N. (1997). The impact of school reform for the middle school years. *Phi Delta Kappan, 78,* 541–550.

Finkenauer, C., Engels R., Meeus W., and Oosterwegal A. (2002). Self and identity in early adolescence: The pains and gains of knowing who and what you are. In T. M. Brinthaupt & R. P. Lipka (Eds.), *Understanding early adolescent self and identity* (pp. 25–56). Albany, NY: State University of New York Press.

Flowers, N., Mertens, S., & Mulhall, P. (2003). Lessons learned from more than a decade of middle grades research. *Middle School Journal, 35*(2), 55–59.

Furrer, C., & Skinner, E. (2003). Sense of relatedness as a factor in children's academic engagement and performance. *Journal of Educational Psychology, 95*(1) 148–162.

Gardner, H. (1983). *Frames of mind: The theory of multiple intelligences.* New York: Basic Books.

Gardner, H. (1995). Reflections on multiple intelligences: Myths and messages. *Phi Delta Kappan, 77*(4), 200–209.

Gardner, H. (2006). *Multiple intelligences: New horizons.* New York: Basic Books

Gardner, H., & Hatch, T. (1989). Multiple intelligences go to school. *Educational Researcher, 18*(8), 4–10.

Giroux, H. A. (1996). *Fugitive cultures: Race violence and youth.* New York: Routledge.

Glasser, W. (1993). *The quality school teacher.* New York: Harper Perennial.

Glasser, W. (1998). *Choice Theory: A new psychology of personal freedom.* New York: Harper Collins.

Goddard, R. D., Tschannen-Moran, M., & Hoy, W. K. (2001). A multilevel examination of the distribution and effects of teacher trust in students and parents in urban elementary schools. *The Elementary School Journal, 102*(1), 3–17.

Goleman, G. (1995). *Emotional intelligence.* New York: Bantam Books.

Goleman, G. (1998). *Working with emotional intelligence.* New York: Bantam Books.

Greer, F. R., & Krebs, N. F. (2006) Optimizing bone health and calcium intakes of infants, children, and adolescents. *Pediatrics, 117*(2), 578–585.

Herbert, J., Stipek, D., & Miles, S. J. (2003). *Gender differences in perceptions of ability in elementary school students: The role of parents, teachers, and achievement.* Paper presented at the annual meeting of the American Educational Research Association, Chicago.

Hinton, S. E. (1967). *The outsiders.* New York: Dell Publishing Co.

Hockenberry-Eaton, M., & Richman, M. J. (1996). Mother and adolescent knowledge of sexual development: The effects of gender, age, and sexual experience. *Adolescence, 31*(121), 35–48.

Hoge, R. D. (1999). *Assessing adolescents in educational, counseling, and other settings.* London: Lawrence Erlbaum Associates.

Intrator, S. M., & Kunzman, R. (2009). Who are adolescents today? Youth voices and what they tell us. In L. Christenbury, R. Bomer, & P. Smagorinsky (Eds.) *Handbook of adolescent literacy research* (pp. 29–47). New York: The Guilford Press.

Johnson, P., & Malow-Iroff, M. (2008). *Adolescents and risk: Making sense of adolescent psychology.* Westport, CT: Praeger.

Jones, D. C., & Crawford, J. K. (2006). The peer appearance culture during adolescence: Gender and body mass variations [Electronic version]. *Journal of Youth and Adolescence, 35*(2), 243–255.

Josselson, R. (1994). The theory of identity development and the question of intervention: An introduction. In S. L Archer (Ed.), *Interventions for adolescent identity development* (pp. 12–28). London: Sage.

Joyce, B., Wolf, J., & Calhoun, E. (1993). *The self-renewing school.* Alexandria, VA: Association for Supervision and Curriculum Development.

Kruczek, T., Alexander, C., & Harris, K. (2005). An after-school program for high-risk middle school students. *Professional School Counseling, 9*(20),160–163.

Langer, J. (2009). Contexts for adolescent literacy. In L. Christenbury, R. Bomer, & P. Smagorinsky (Eds.), *Handbook of adolescent literacy research* (pp. 49–64). New York: The Guilford Press.

Larson, R., Richards, M., Meneta, G., & Duckett, E. (1996). Changes in adolescents' daily interactions with their families from age 10–18: Disengagement and transformation. *Developmental Psychology, 32,* 744–754.

Leamnson, R. (1999). *Think about teaching and learning.* Sterling, VA: Stylus Publishing.

Lee. V. E., & Smith, J. B. (1993). Effects of school restructuring on the achievement and engagement of middle-grades students. *Sociology of Education, 66*(3), 164–187.

L'Esperance, M., & Farrington, V. T. (2004). Using data for significant improvement. *Middle Matters Online, 2*(3). Retrieved from http://www.naesp.org/Middle_Matters.aspx

L'Esperance, M., Farrington, V. T., & Fryer, A. (2005). Creating significant middle schools in the age of accountability. *Middle Ground, 10*(9), 35–39.

L'Esperance, M., & Farrington, V. T. (2007). The search for significance: Leadership lessons from the field. *NC Middle School Journal.* Retrieved January 28, 2009, from http://www.ncmsa.net/journal/PDF/Feb08/Strengthening-middle-level-education.pdf

L'Esperance, M., Strahan, D., Farrington, V. T, & Anderson, P. (2003). *Raising achievement: Project genesis, a significant school model.* Westerville, OH: National Middle School Association.

Linneback, E. A., & Pintrich, P. R. (2002). Motivation as an enabler for academic success. *School Psychology Review, 31*(3) 313–327.

Lopez, C., & DuBois, D. (2005). Peer victimization and rejection: Investigation of an integrative model of effects on emotional, behavioral, and academic adjustment in early adolescence. *Journal of Clinical Child and Adolescent Psychology, 34*(1), 25–36.

Mack, D. E., Strong, H. A., Kowalski, K. C., & Crocker, P. R. E. (2007). Does friendship matter? An examination of social physique anxiety in adolescence [Electronic version]. *Journal of Applied Social Psychology, 37*(6), 1248–1264.

Magen, Z. (1998). *Exploring adolescent happiness: Commitment, purpose, and fulfillment.* London: Sage.

Manning, M. A. (2007). Re-framing how we see student self-concept. *Education Digest: Essential Readings Condensed for Quick Review, 72*(8), 36–41. Retrieved from http://web.ebscohost.com/ehost

Masci. F. (2008). *Time for time and task and quality instruction. Middle School Journal, 40*(2), 33–41.

McCombs, B. L., and Marzano, R. J. (1990). Putting the self in self-regulated learning: The self as agent in integrating will and skill. *Educational Psychologist, 25*(1) 51–69.

McDevitt, T. M., & Ormrod, J. E. (2007). *Child development and education* (3rd ed.). Columbus, OH: Pearson.

Mee, C. S. (1997). *2,000 Voices: Young adolescents' perceptions and curriculum implications.* Columbus, OH: National Middle School Association.

Moneta, G., Schneiderb B., & Csikszentmihalyi, M. (2001) A longitudinal study of the self-concept and experiential components of self-worth and affect across adolescence. *Applied Developmental Science, 5*(3), 125–142.

Moran, S., Kornhaber, M., & Gardner, H. (2006). Orchestrating multiple intelligences. *Educational Leadership,* 22–27.

National Center for Chronic Disease Prevention and Health Promotion. (2006). School health guidelines for student nutrition. Retrieved January 31, 2008, from http://www.cdc.gov/HealthyYouth/nutrition/guidelines/summary.htm

National Middle School Association (2003). *This we believe: Successful schools for young adolescents.* Westerville, OH: Author.

National Middle School Association (2005, July). *Initial level teacher preparation standards.* Retrieved from http://www.nmsa.org/ProfessionalPreparation/ NMSAStandards/tabid/374/Default.aspx

Neinstein, L. S. (2004). Adolescent health curriculum: Puberty—normal growth and development. Retrieved from http://web.ebscohost.com/ehost/

Newcomb, M. D. (1996). Adolescence: Pathologizing a normal process. *Counseling Psychologist, 24,* 482–491.

Neufeldt, V. (Ed.) (1997). *Webster's new world college dictionary.* New York: Macmillan.

O'Dea, J., & Abraham, S. (1999). Onset of disordered eating attitudes and behaviors in early adolescence: Interplay of pubertal status, gender, weight, and age. *Adolescence, 34,* 671–679.

Ogbu, J. U. (1991). Cultural diversity and school experience. In C. E. Walsh (Ed.), *Literacy as praxis: Culture, language, and pedagogy* (pp. 25–50). Norwood, NJ: Ablex.

Operario D., Tschann J. M., Flores E., & Bridges M. (2006). Brief report: Associations of parental warmth, peer support, and gender with adolescent emotional distress. *Journal of Adolescence, 29,* 299–305.

Paris, S. G., & Paris, A. H. (2001). Classroom applications of research on self-regulated learning. *Educational Psychologist, 36*(2), 89–101.

Passaro, P. D., Moon, M., Wiest, D. J. & Wong, E. H. (2004). A model for school psychology practice: Addressing the needs of students with emotional and behavioral challenges through the use of an in-school support program and reality therapy. *Adolescence, 39*(155), 503–509.

Payne, M. (2005). An inviting, supportive, and safe environment. In T. Erb (Ed.), *This we believe in action: Implementing successful middle level schools* (pp. 35–42) Westerville, OH: National Middle School Association.

Piaget, J. (1970). *Science of education and the psychology of the child.* New York: Penguin Books.

Piaget, J. (1972). Intellectual evolution from adolescence to adulthood. *Human Development, 15,* 1–12.

Picucci, A. C., Brownson, A., Kahlert, R., & Sobel, A. (2004). Middle school concept helps high poverty schools become high-performing schools. *Middle School Journal, 36*(1), 4–11.

Pinker, S. (1997). *How the mind works.* New York: Penguin Books.

Pinker, S. (2007). *The stuff of thought: Language as a window into human nature.* New York: Viking Penguin Books.

Purkey, W. W., & Strahan, D. B. (1986). *Positive discipline: A pocketful of ideas.* Columbus, OH: National Middle School Association.

Qualter, P., Whiteley, H. E., Hutchinson, J. M., & Pope, D. J. (2007). Supporting the development of emotional intelligence competencies to ease the transition from primary to high school. *Educational Psychology in Practice, 23*(1), 79–95.

Quintana, S. M. (1998). Children's developmental understanding of ethnicity and race. *Applied and Preventative Psychology,* 7(1), 27–45.

Ravenscroft, A. (2007). Promoting thinking and conceptual change with digital dialogue games. *Journal of Computer Assisted Learning, 23,* 453–465.

Ravitch, D., & Viteritti, J. P. (2003). Toxic lessons: Children and popular culture. In D. Ravitch & J. Viteritti (Eds), *Marketing sex and violence to America's chidren* (pp. 1–18). Baltimore: The John Hopkins University Press.

Rhodes, J. A., & Robnolt, V. J. (2009). Digital literacies in the classroom. In L. Christenbury, R. Bomer, & P. Smagorinsky (Eds.) *Handbook of adolescent literacy research* (pp. 153–169). New York: The Guilford Press.

Roesser, R. W., Eccles, J. S., & Sameroff, A. J. (2000). School as a context of early adolescents' academic and social-emotional development: A summary of research findings. *The Elementary School Journal, 100*(5), 454–471.

Rojas-Drummond, S. M., Albarran, C. D., & Littleton, K. S. (2008). Collaboration, creativity and the co-construction of oral and written texts. *Thinking Skills and Creativity, 3,* 177–191.

Routledge, R. B., Mani, P. S., Pence, A. R., & Hoskins, M. L. (2001). Exploring the role of family and peers in adolescent self-representation: Toward a dialectical perspective. *Child and Youth Care Forum, 30*(1), 35–54.

Scales, P. C. (1996). A responsive ecology for positive young adolescent development. *Clearing House,* 69, 226–230.

Scales, P. C. (1999). Increasing service learning's impact on middle school students. *Middle School Journal, 30*(5), 40–44.

Schunk, D. (2003). Self-efficacy for reading and writing: Influence of modeling, goal setting, and self-evaluation. *Reading and Writing Quarterly, 19,* 159–172.

Smart, M. S., & Smart, R. C. (1973). *Adolescence.* New York: Macmillan Publishing Co.

Smetana, J., & Turiel, E. (2003). Moral development during adolescence. In G. Adams, & M. Berzonsky (Eds.), *Blackwell handbook of adolescence.* Malden, MA: Blackwell Publishing Company.

Smith, D. B. (2005). Accountability for academics and social responsibility through service learning. *Middle School Journal, 36*(4), 20-25.

Smith, S., & Donnerstein, E. (2003). The problem of exposure: Violence, sex, drugs, & alcohol. In D. Ravitch & J. Viteritti (Eds.), *Kid stuff: Marketing sex and violence to America's children* (pp. 65–95). Baltimore: Johns Hopkins University Press.

Smith-McIlwain, K. (2005). *A study of trust in the motivation and academic performance of disengaged writers.* Greensboro, NC: University of North Carolina Greensboro.

Strahan, D. (1988). Life on the margins: How academically at-risk early adolescents view themselves and school. *Journal of Early Adolescence, 8*(4), 373–390.

Strahan, D. B. (1997). *Mindful learning: Teaching self-discipline and academic achievement.* Durham, NC: Carolina Academic Press.

Strahan, D. B. (2008). Successful teachers develop academic momentum with reluctant students. *Middle School Journal, 39*(5), 4–12.

Strahan, D. B., Faircloth, C. V., Cope, M. & Hundley, S. (2007). Exploring the dynamics of academic reconnections: A case study of middle school teachers' efforts and students' responses. *Middle Grades Research Journal, 2*(2), 19–41.

Strahan, D., & Layell, K. (2006). Connecting caring and action through responsive teaching: How one team accomplished success in a struggling middle school. *The Clearing House, 9*(3), 147–154.

Strahan, D., Smith, T., McElrath, M., & Toole, C. (2001). Profiles in caring: Teachers who create learning communities in their classrooms. In T. Dickinson (Ed.) *Reinventing the Middle School* (pp. 96–116). New York: Routledge Press.

The Center for Disease Control. (2007). *Healthy youth.* Retrieved November 19, 2008, from http://www.cdc.gov/healthyyouth/nutrition/guidelines/summary.htm

The Federal Interagency Forum on Child and Family Statistics. (2008). *America's children in brief: Key national indicators of well-being.* Retrieved April 27, 2008, from http://www.childstats.gov/americaschildren/glance.asp

Thinklab, (1974). Chicago: Science Research Associates.

Tobin, K. G., & Capie, W. (2006). Relationships between formal reasoning ability, locus of control, academic engagement, and integrated process skill achievement. *Journal of Research in Science Teaching 19*(2), 113–121.

Tomlinson, C. A. (2003). *Fulfilling the promise of the differentiated classroom.* Alexandria, VA: Association for Supervision and Curriculum Development.

Tse, L. (1999). Finding a place to be: Ethnic identity exploration of Asian Americans. *Adolescence, 34*(133), 121–138.

Van Hoose, J. (1983). Television: A major cause of undesirable behavior. *NASSP Bulletin, 67*(463), 97–101.

Van Hoose, J. (1991). The ultimate goal: A/A across the day. *Midpoints, 2*(1). Columbus, OH: National Middle School Association.

Van Hoose, J., & Strahan, D. (1988). *Young adolescent development and school practices: Promoting harmony.* Columbus, OH: National Middle School Association.

Van Hoose, J., Strahan, D., & L'Esperance, M. (2001). *Promoting harmony. Young adolescent development and school practices.* Westerville, OH: National Middle School Association

Vygotsky, L. S. (1978). *Mind in society: The development of higher mental psychological processes.* Cambridge, MA: MIT Press.

Vygotsky, L. S. (1986). *Thought and language* (translation newly revised and edited by Alex Kozulin). Cambridge, MA: Massachusetts Institute of Technology.

Walter, S. M., Lambie, G. W., & Ngazimbi, E. E. (2008). A Choice Theory counseling group succeeds with middle school students who displayed disciplinary problems. *Middle School Journal, 40*(2), 4–12.

Weaver, C. M. (2002) Adolescence: The period of dramatic bone growth. *Endocrine, 17*(1), 43–48.

Whetstone, L. M., Morrissey, S. L., & Cummings, D. M. (2007). Children at risk: The association between perceived weight status and suicidal thoughts and attempts in middle school youth. *Journal of School Health, 77*(2), 59–66.

Willis, J. (2007). Cooperative learning is a brain turn-on. *Middle School Journal, 38*(4), 4–13.

Wood, K. D., Roser, N. L., & Martinez, M. (2001). Collaborative literacy: Lessons learned from literature. *The Reading Teacher, 55*(2), 102–111.

Woolfolk, A. E. (1998). *Educational psychology* (7th ed.), Boston: Allyn and Bacon.

Wyatt, T. J., & Peterson, F. L. (2005). Risky business: Exploring adolescent risk-taking behavior. *Journal of School Health, 75*(6).

Xiaojia, G., Elder, G. H. Jr., Regenrus, M., & Cox, C. (2001). Pubertal transitions, perceptions of being overweight, and adolescents' psychological maladjustment: Gender and ethnic differences [Electronic version]. *Social Psychology Quarterly, 64*(4), 363–375.

Zapata, L. B., Bryant, C. A., McDermott, R. J., & Hefelfinger, J. A. (2008). Dietary & physical activity behaviors of middle school youth: The youth physical activity and nutrition survey [Electronic version]. *Journal of School Health, 78*(1), 9–18.

Zimmerman, B. J. (1989). Models of self-regulated learning and academic achievement. In B. J. Zimmerman & D. H. Schunk (Eds.), *Self-regulated learning and academic achievement: Theory, research, and practice* (pp. 1–25). New York: Springer and Verlag.

Zimmerman, B. J., Bonner, S., & Kovach, R. (1996). *Developing self-regulated learners: Beyond achievement to self-efficacy.* Washington, DC: American Psychological Association.

Zoss, M. (2009). Visual arts and literacy. In L. Christenbury, R. Bomer, & P. Smagorinsky (Eds.) *Handbook of adolescent literacy research* (pp. 183–196). New York: The Guilford Press.

CPSIA information can be obtained at www.ICGtesting.com
Printed in the USA
BVOW062314230412

288426BV00004B/1/P